COOKING IN
EUROPE, 1650–1850

**Recent Titles in The Greenwood Press
"Daily Life Through History" Series**

Along the Mississippi
George S. Pabis

Immigrant America, 1820–1870
James M. Bergquist

Pre-Columbian Native America
Clarissa W. Confer

Post-Cold War
Stephen A. Bourque

The New Testament
James W. Ermatinger

The Hellenistic Age: From Alexander to Cleopatra
James Allan Evans

Imperial Russia
Greta Bucher

The Greenwood Encyclopedia of Daily Life in America, Four Volumes
Randall M. Miller, general editor

Civilians in Wartime Twentieth-Century Europe
Nicholas Atkin, Editor

Ancient Egyptians, Revised Edition
Bob Brier and Hoyt Hobbs

Civilians in Wartime Latin America:
From the Wars of Independence to the Central American Civil Wars
Pedro Santoni, editor

Science and Technology in Modern European Life
Guillaume de Syon

COOKING IN

EUROPE,
1650–1850

Ivan Day

The Greenwood Press "Daily Life Through History" Series
Cooking Up History
Kenneth Albala, Series Editor

12/08

Greenwood Press
Westport, Connecticut • London

Library of Congress Cataloging-in-Publication Data

Day, Ivan.
  Cooking in Europe, 1650–1850 / Ivan Day.
      p. cm. — (The Greenwood Press "Daily life through history" series.
Cooking up history, ISSN 1080–4749)
  Includes bibliographical references and index.
  ISBN 978–0–313–34624–8 (alk. paper)
  1. Cookery, European—History. I. Title.
  TX723.5.A1D388 2009
  641.594—dc22   2008029724

British Library Cataloguing in Publication Data is available.

Library of Congress Catalog Card Number: 2008029724
ISBN: 978–0–313–34624–8
ISSN: 1080–4749

First published in 2009

Greenwood Press, 88 Post Road West, Westport, CT 06881
An imprint of Greenwood Publishing Group, Inc.
www.greenwood.com

Printed in the United States of America

The paper used in this book complies with the
Permanent Paper Standard issued by the National
Information Standards Organization (Z39.48–1984).

10 9 8 7 6 5 4 3 2 1

Copyright Acknowledgments

The author and publisher gratefully acknowledge permission for use of the following
material:

All illustrations are from Ivan Day's personal collection of historic cookbooks and all photo
credits are to him.

The publisher has done its best to make sure the instructions and/or recipes in this book are
correct. However, users should apply judgment and experience when preparing recipes, especially parents and teachers working with young people. The publisher accepts no responsibility for the outcome of any recipe included in this volume.

❧ CONTENTS

❧ LIST OF RECIPES

Vegetables and Fungi

Eggs and Dairy

Sauces

Savory Pies and Pastries

Starches, Pastas, and Legumes

Ices

Drinks

THE REIGN OF LOUIS XV TO THE FRENCH REVOLUTION, 1750–1800

Soups

Meat

Poultry and Game

Fish and Seafood

Savory Pastries

Starches and Pastas

Eggs and Dairy

Sauces

Breads and Cakes

Sweet Pastries and Puddings

THE REIGN OF NAPOLEON TO THE VICTORIAN ERA, 1800–1850

Sweet Pastries

Jellies and Ices

GLOSSARY

ADUBOS: Old Portuguese name for a mixture of spices and seasonings.

ALEXANDERS: (*Smyrnium olusatrum*). Salad herb related to celery.

BABA: Yeast cake of Polish origin.

BARBERRIES: (*Berberis vulgaris*). Bright red acid berries of the European barberry.

BARD: Sheet of pork or bacon fat.

BARM: Yeast obtained from brewing beer.

BIGARADE ORANGE: (*Citrus aurantium*). Bitter, or Seville, orange.

BISCOTTINI: Little biscuits, sometimes ship's biscuit.

BISQUE: A rich soup or stew made with pigeon or crayfish.

BOMBE: A molded ice cream in the shape of a ball or artillery shell.

BOUILLON: A stock used as a basis for making soups.

BOTARGO: Salted tuna or grey mullet roe.

BORAGE: (*Borago officianalis*). Salad herb with bright blue flowers and a cucumber flavor.

BUGLOSS: (*Echium vulgare*). A relative of borage with bright blue and pink edible flowers.

BRAISING PAN: A large pan with a lid that can be filled with burning embers.

BRAWN: Boar meat pickled in a liquid called a souse, which consisted of a mixture of wine, water, vinegar, and spices.

BRIGNOLLE PRUNES: A dried plum from Brignolle in southern France.

BROACH: A small spit or skewer.

BROOK LIME: (*Veronica beccabunga*). An aquatic plant often used in spring salads.

BROOM BUDS: (*Sarothamnus scoparius*). The immature buds of the wild broom bush.

CANTUCCI: A type of almond biscuit from Italy.

CARDOONS: (*Cynara cardunculus*). The blanched stems of an artichoke relative.

CAUDLE: A sauce made with egg yolks, wine, and sugar.

CAUL: A fatty membrane enclosing the inner organs.

CHAFING DISH: A small brazier for burning charcoal.

CHARCOAL STEWING STOVE: A raised platform containing a number of charcoal braziers.

CITRON: (*Citrus medica*). A large lemon-like fruit preserved as a candy.

COCKSCOMBS: The fleshy growths on cockerel's heads, often used as a garnish.

COMFITS: Sugar coated nuts, seeds, and spices.

CONSOMMÉ: A clear, transparent soup or stock.

CORDIAL: A strong alcoholic spirit flavored with herbs and spices.

COULIS: A meat or fish concentrate used in seventeenth and eighteenth century cooking.

CREAM OF BARBADOS: A liqueur flavored with citrons.

CUBEBS: (*Piper cubeba*). A species of pepper used in medieval cookery.

DAUBIÈRE: French name for a braising pan.

ESPAGNOLE: A rich brown sauce.

FIRE SHOVEL: A long-handled shovel for putting coals on the fire. Sometimes used in place of a salamander (see salamander).

FOIE GRAS: Goose livers.

FRISELLE: A ring-shaped dry, crisp bread.

FURZE: (*Ulex europeaus*). A thorny shrub commonly found on wasteland throughout Europe.

GALANTINE: A cinnamon-flavored sauce. Also a boiled meat dish encased in gelatin.

GALINGALE: (*Alpinia officinarum*). A spicy root related to ginger from Indonesia.

GALLIPOT: A ceramic storage pot.

GRAINS OF PARADISE: (*Aframomum melegueta*). The seeds of an African relative of ginger.

GRATIN: Originally a seasoned meat paste. More recently a dish covered in toasted breadcrumbs.

JUS: The juices that exude from roasted meat (see recipe 177).

KATENRAUCHWURST: A German smoked sausage with a coarse texture.

KUGELHOPF: A yeast cake baked in a spiral mold.

LARDING: The process of sewing strips of bacon fat into lean meat and game.

LARDOONS: Strips of bacon fat.

LAZEROLE MEDLARS: (*Crataegus azarolus*). An acid-fruited hawthorn more usually known in Italy as the azarole.

LEVAIN: A fermenting dough mixture or sourdough starter.

LEVANTINE DATES: Dates from the Middle East (Levant).

MACE: (*Myristica fragrans*). An aromatic spice consisting of the bladelike covering of the nutmeg.

MALMSEY: Originally a Greek wine made from Malvasia grapes.

MALVASIA: A sweet wine made from Malvasia grapes.

MANCHET: A small white loaf or roll.

MARASCHINO: A spirit distilled from bitter cherries.

MARMITE: A cast-iron cooking pot.

MARROW FAT: A rich fat extracted from bones like the tibia of oxen and calves.

MIGNONETTE: An herb and spice mixture (see recipe 29).

MIGNONETTE PEPPER: A mixture of coarsely ground white and black pepper.

MINESTRA: A thick soup.

MITONNAGE: Stock or bouillon.

OFFICE: A French term for a confectionery room or pantry.

ORANGADO: Candied orange peel.

ORTOLAN: (*Emberiza hortulana*). A bird related to the bunting.

PALATE: The meat removed from the roof of the mouth of oxen and calves.

PANADA: A thickening agent made from flour or bread.

PERFETTO AMORE: A bright red Italian liqueur flavored with lemon and spices.

PASSIENCE: (*Rumex alpine*). A large-leaved plant used for making fritters.

PÂTISSIER: French name for pastry cook.

PÂTE D'OFFICE: A hard inedible pastry made from flour, water, and sugar used for making table ornaments.

PENNYROYAL: (*Mentha pulegium*). An aromatic herb related to mint.

PIÈCES MONTÉES: Large ornamental table centerpieces, often architectural in form.

PIPKIN: A three-legged saucepan used for cooking over embers. Sometimes also called a posnet.

PORTUGAL ORANGES: (*Citrus aurantium, var. Dulcis*). Sweet oranges.

POTTAGE: An old name for a soup or broth.

POTTLE: Two quarts.

PROVATURA: An Italian cheese, closely related to mozzarella.

PURSLANE: (*Portulacea oleracea*). A succulent salad herb.

RAGOÛT: A rich stew.

RATAFIA: An alcoholic drink made by infusing fruit and sugar in brandy.

RECADO: An old Spanish name for a mixture of herbs and other seasonings

ROCAMBOLES: (*Allium scorodoprasum*). A member of the onion family, formerly much used in salads.

ROSOLIO: Originally a bright yellow liqueur from Turin, distilled from various sundew species (*Drosera* spp.).

ROUX: A liaison of flour cooked in butter used as a thickening agent.

SALAMANDER: A kind of cast-iron poker with a large round end that could be heated red hot and used for toasting food.

SALPICOENS: A type of large preserved sausage made in Portugal.

SALSA: Italian and Spanish word signifying *sauce*.

SALSIFY: (*Tragopogon porrifolius*). A root vegetable shaped like a long thin carrot.

SAMPHIRE: (*Crithmum maritimum*). A coastal plant common throughout Southern Europe. The leaves were preserved as a pickle.

SAPORE: A sauce-like relish.

SCAROLA: An unidentified Italian salad herb, probably a type of chicory or endive.

SCORZONERA: A variety of salsify.

SIPPETS: Small pieces of toasted bread, usually triangular in shape.

SKIRRETS: (*Sium sisarum*). A sweet-rooted vegetable related to the parsnip.

SOPPRESSATA: A pressed meat.

SORBETIÈRE: A pewter, tin, or copper freezing pot.

SPANISH BREAD: A sponge biscuit.

SPUN SUGAR: Sugar heated to caramel and spun into threads for decoration.

STOCKFISH: Salted members of the cod family.

STOFFADO: A culinary term with various meanings, but most usually a rich stew cooked over a stove.

TAMMY-CLOTH OR TAMIS: A fine cloth used for straining liquids.

TARALLI: A round, dry, crisp bread made in southern Italy.

TARANTELLO: Salted tuna belly.

TOKAY: A sweet Hungarian wine made from Tokaj grapes.

TOUR À PÂTE: A special work station used by a pastry cook.

TRIONFI: Sugar table sculpture.

VELOUTÉ: A smooth, highly flavored white sauce.

VERJUICE: The lightly fermented juice of sour, unripe grapes or crab apples. Much used in the early modern period as an acidic flavoring and meat tenderizer.

WESTPHALIAN BROWN CABBAGE: A kind of kale similar to modern curly kale.

ZUPPA: Italian name for a thick soup-like dish; sometimes a sweet dish based on bread.

𝒜 SERIES FOREWORD

The beasts have memory, judgment and all the faculties and passions
of our mind, in a certain degree; but no beast is a cook.

This quip by the eighteenth-century Scottish biographer James Boswell
defines the essence of humanity in a way his contemporaries would have
found humorous but also thought provoking. It is neither an immortal soul,
reason, nor powers of abstraction that separate us from animals, but the simple ability to use fire to transform our daily fare into something more palatable
and nutritious. We are nothing more than cooking animals. Archaeological
evidence bears this out; it is Homo sapiens, our distant Neanderthal relatives,
whose sites offer the earliest incontrovertible evidence of cooking. From those
distant times down to the present, the food we eat and how it is prepared has
become the decisive factor in the survival of both individuals and whole civi-
lizations, so what better way to approach the subject of history than through
the bubbling cauldron?

Growing and preparing food has also been the occupation of the vast major-
ity of men and women who ever lived. To understand humans, we should
naturally begin with the food that constitutes the fabric of our existence. Yet
every culture arrives at different solutions, uses different crops and cooking
methods, and invents what amount to unique cuisines. These are to some
extent predetermined by geography and technology, and a certain amount of
luck. Nonetheless every cuisine is a practical and artistic expression of the

culture that created it. It embodies the values and aspirations each society, its world outlook as well as its history.

This series examines cooking as an integral part of important epochs in history, both as a way to examine daily life for women and men who cooked, but also as a way to explore the experiences of people who ate what was served. Cookbooks are thus treated here as primary source documents that students can interpret just as they might a legal text, literary or artistic work, or any other historical evidence. Through them we are afforded a glimpse, sometimes of what transpired in the great halls of the powerful, but also in more modest households. Unlike most forms of material culture, we can also recreate these dishes today to get an immediate and firsthand experience of the food that people in the past relished. I heartily encourage you to taste the past in these recipes, keeping in mind good taste is not universal and some things are simply impossible to make today. But a good number of dishes, I assure you, will both surprise and delight.

We begin the series with volumes stretching from ancient times to the twentieth century, including European and American regions, written by experts in culinary history who have done a superb job of interpreting the historical texts while remaining faithful to their integrity. Each is designed to appeal to the novice cook, with technical and historical terms amply defined, and timely advice proffered for the adventurous time traveler in the kitchen. I hope your foray into the foods of the past is nothing less than an absolute delight.

Ken Albala
University of the Pacific

☙ PREFACE

It is a mistake to assume that because early cooks did not have all the conveniences of a modern kitchen, their cooking techniques and equipment must have been primitive. Anyone who has compared the taste of food cooked in a microwave oven (hi-tech cookery) with that broiled skillfully over a charcoal grill (Neolithic cooking) will tell you that food is not necessarily improved by advancing technology. Take the subject of freezing for instance. Eighteenth- and nineteenth-century confectioners were capable of making ice creams of extraordinary sophistication that were as good as, and often better than, those served in a top restaurant today—and all without resorting to an electrical freezer or refrigerator. Cooking with an open fire, too, was a remarkably skilled operation, with a huge range of well-designed equipment available to help the cook produce dishes of astonishing quality.

Some of the historical meals given as examples in this book would present a massive challenge to a well-equipped modern restaurant kitchen. For instance, the 1660 Christmas dinner on pages 36–37 consists of 40 different dishes. Yet gargantuan feasts like this were produced regularly in kitchens where there was no hot water, and by cooks who frequently worked by candlelight.

This collection of recipes is intended for those who would like to try making for themselves some of the dishes that were popular during this critical period in European history. Most of them are not difficult, though a number of more challenging recipes are included to illustrate the scope and technical dexterity of these early kitchen workers. Recreating historical dishes is rather like attempting to perform early music. Period recipes, like early musical scores, do not have all the information that we would nowadays expect. Quantities are often vague; cooking times and temperatures are frequently not even discussed. However, with the application of a little common sense, these difficulties can easily be overcome and good results can be achieved from most early recipes. In my experience the only ones that do not work are those where there has been a careless printing error or a mistake in copying a transcription.

When I first started cooking from period recipes over 40 years ago, it was very difficult to locate some of the more obscure ingredients. Nowadays the Internet has changed that and many of these foodstuffs are easily purchased with a few clicks of a mouse. Reproduction historical culinary equipment is also readily available for those adventurous enough to venture out of the comfort zone of their modern kitchens. A list of Internet suppliers of ingredients and equipment can be found in the appendix.

The period covered by this book was the age of Newton, Voltaire, Adam Smith, and Diderot, an epoch when rationalism triumphed over medieval worldviews. This intellectual revolution even found its way into the kitchen. Cookbooks became more organized, recipes more precise, and equipment more scientific—the pressure-cooker, thermometer, and saccharometer all found a useful place on the kitchen shelf at this time. It was also a period of extraordinary artistic achievement and this too was reflected in the work of the humble cook. Many of the culinary professionals of this period had artistic skills of a very high standard. For instance, confectioners could produce table sculptures out of sugar paste that were as technically good as those carved in marble or modeled in porcelain. Pastry cooks could ornament pies with complex decorative motifs that were as beautiful as those of contemporary plasterwork. The great French pastry cook Antonin Carême insisted that "the fine arts are five in number—painting, sculpture, poetry, music, architecture—whose main branch is confectionery."[1] Many of the impressive illustrations in this work will demonstrate the truth of Carême's statement.

This book covers a period in which European cookery underwent extraordinary transformation. The recipes are divided into three sections and have been chosen to illuminate how these crucial changes unfolded. Chapter 1 covers the period 1650–1750, a time when French high-class cuisine spread rapidly throughout Europe. This was the era of the baroque feast and dishes tended to be lavish and meals complex. Many of the books published at this time were written by high-status cooks who worked in princely households, and their recipes show off the magnificence of court food culture. Signature dishes of this period are sumptuous stews like the olio (recipe 29) and heavily ornamented pastries (recipes 59 and 60). Chapter 2 consists of recipes published from 1750–1800, a time when cookbook writers targeted their books more and more at female readers who wanted practical and less costly recipes. In some countries, like Germany and England, increasing numbers of women started to write cookbooks for a growing middle-class readership. In France, where cookbook authors remained exclusively male, recipes became more refined and rational in structure. Even cooking at court became a little simpler and rustic as dishes like garbure (recipe 105) became fashionable. Chapter 3 roughly covers the period after the French Revolution and the early decades of industrialization, from 1800 to 1850. It was a time when foods and beverages formerly considered luxuries, like white bread, tea, chocolate, and ices, became available lower down the social scale. Cooking equipment started to be mass-produced and attractive molded foods, which a century before only graced the tables of the wealthy, became much more widespread. At a very high social level, food reached new heights of opulence under the influence of French cooks like Carême. By the 1850s even cookbooks for working-class families were appearing on the scene.

The choice of recipes has been a personal one. The cooking literature of this period is vast and rich in scope, so it has not been an easy task making the final selection. A few luxurious dishes have been included as interesting examples of high-status dining, but it is not expected that readers will attempt these. Most recipes, however, are perfectly practical today and hopefully will open up a few unusual culinary byways for the modern cook to explore.

Bringing history to life through cooking the food of our ancestors can be a rewarding and revelatory experience. A great number of the classic and traditional European dishes that we enjoy today started as ideas in the minds of nameless cooks and housewives who lived centuries ago. However, the turmoil of history has meant that many other great dishes have been lost on the way. A number of these long forgotten foods are well worth reviving and will hopefully be found in these pages. Good cooking and *bon appétit!*

✍ ACKNOWLEDGMENTS

In assembling this book, I have been inspired by the work of many scholars of culinary history and dining. Foremost among these have been Ken Albala, Claudio Benporat, Peter Brears, Maureen Cassidy-Geiger, Meredith Chilton, the late Alan Davidson, Jean-Louis Flandrin, Giovanni Giusti, Alain Gruber, Karen Hess, Christopher Hartop, Philip and Mary Hyman, Tom Jaine, Deborah Krohn, Gilly Lehmann, Gillian Riley, Terence Scully, Roy Strong, June de Schino, Selma Schwartz, Barbara Wheaton, John Whitehead, Marleen Willebrands, C. Anne Wilson, and Carolyn Young. Invaluable help and advice with recipe translation has been generously forthcoming from David Corrie, Tom Hall, Gillian Riley, Luc Vanackere, and Gill Whitehead. Other friends and colleagues who have been generous with their encouragement and advice have been Robert Appelbaum, Heston Blumenthal, Janet Clarke, Jane Hasell–McCosh, Michiko Nozawa, and Robin Weir.

I am also very grateful to the staff of the Special Collections at the Brotherton Library of the University of Leeds, Barbara Wheaton at the Schlesinger Library of the University of Harvard, the staff of Kendal Record Office, and the staff at the British Library in London. Finally I would like to thank my editor, Ken Albala, for his infectious enthusiasm and Wendi Schnaufer at the Greenwood Press for her encouragement and enduring patience. Most of all I would like to thank my late friend Gervase Markham, modern namesake and descendent of the celebrated Jacobean author on cookery, who sadly died while this book was being written. It is affectionately dedicated to his memory.

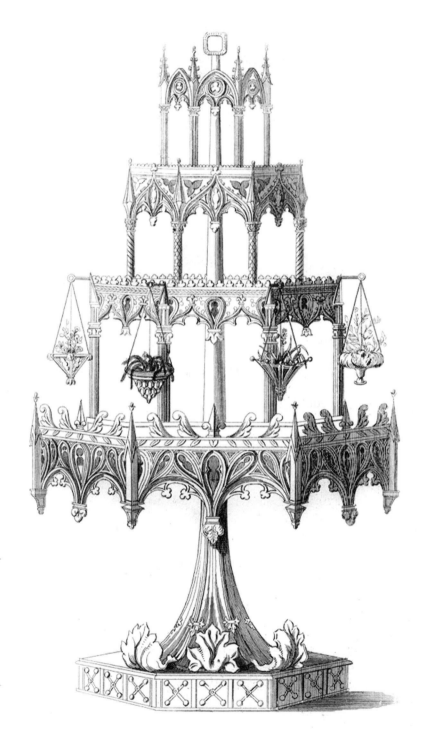

A French pièce montée *(table ornament) made of sugar paste, 1846. These techni-cally demanding edible decorations were a common feature of high-class dinner tables. They were the descendents of the sugar sculpture of the Italian renaissance.*

1
🦅 INTRODUCTION: FROM THE BAROQUE ERA TO THE VICTORIAN AGE

New culinary procedures

- The international triumph of French court cooking
- New ingredients: potato, tomato, chocolate, tea, coffee, pineapple
- Science in the kitchen: artificial freezing
- Improving culinary equipment
- The table setting introduced

During the two centuries covered by this book, unprecedented changes took place in the foodways and dining habits of European society. Of these, the most important was a dramatic shift in culinary taste led by the exuberant creativity of French cooks. At the beginning of this period, meat and fish dishes seasoned with spices, sugar, and fruit were popular. These foods, widespread since the medieval period, were ultimately derived from Arab and Persian culinary traditions. Spicy soups of chicken and prunes, pies filled with meatballs cooked in a sauce of sour grapes, and crab seasoned with spice and gooseberries were typical of this culinary style. Floral waters and candied peels were also frequently included in meat dishes and sauces, particularly in Spain and Italy. Sugar was widely used as a seasoning to enhance the flavors of savory dishes. Ravioli, for instance, was dredged with grated Parmesan cheese, powdered sugar, and cinnamon. Sugar was also frequently combined with acidic fruit juices to create a sweet-sour effect in meat and fish dishes.

Some important changes had already taken place in the sixteenth century, when a number of spices popular in medieval cookery, like cubebs, galingale, and grains of paradise, disappeared from the kitchen cupboard. However, the gradual movement away from the sweet-sour culinary style did not really begin in France until after 1630. Unfortunately no French recipe books were published between 1560 and 1651, so it is not possible to gauge exactly when this trend began.

During the 1650s, cookbooks started to emerge from the Paris printing presses after a hundred years of silence, and it is evident that immense advances had taken place in French cooking. As will be seen in the first recipe section of this book, the old mixtures of sweet and sour were still to be found in these new collections, but alongside them there were subtle new flavor combinations based on herbs, mushrooms, and savory elements. The use of spices was more restrained; cinnamon, for instance, tended to be restricted to sweet dishes.

In 1660, a new culinary preparation known as *coulis* was described for the first time.[1] This ready-prepared meat or fish concentrate, with its thickening of flour and intense flavoring, became a signature feature of the new style of French cooking, allowing the cook to heighten the tang of a sauce or soup in a moment with a quick stir of a wooden spoon. *Roux*, a liaison of flour and fat used as a thickening, was another new addition to the cook's repertoire of stock ingredients. In the old days, sauces and soups had always been thickened with breadcrumbs or pounded almonds. It took about a hundred years for these innovations to completely transform French cuisine and sweep away all remnants of lingering medieval taste. By the 1750s French cookbooks had been purged of old-fashioned recipes, though some of these lingered in the cookery traditions of other nations.

Another great French innovation was the foundation of what is often called the modular system of cooking. This methodical approach allowed a dish to be assembled quickly from ready-prepared ingredients that were always kept at hand. Little ceramic pots of roux, stockpots of simmering *bouillon* (stock), and jars of flavor-rich coulis were standard in all well-organized French kitchens. This afforded tremendous flexibility to the cook, giving him scope to improvise new dishes and combinations of flavors with minimum effort. In the later eighteenth century, coulis was displaced by two important stock sauces—*velouté* (white sauce) and *espagnole* (brown sauce). These were freshly made up every morning and used as a basis for preparing many other sauces and for adding flavor, color, and texture to a huge variety of dishes.

It must be understood that these changes took place at a very high social level and were initially confined to the kitchens of the powerful and wealthy. Foreign ambassadors and visitors to the court of King Louis XIV (1643–1715) were particularly impressed with the lavish hospitality and the innovative new style of cooking emanating from the royal kitchens. Dining and entertainments at this court were on a monumental scale and dishes were often rich in expensive ingredients like truffles and morels. By the early decades of the eighteenth century, most other European courts had adopted the new style of dining. In princely palaces from Stockholm to Dresden, high-status French cooking had displaced old-fashioned court cuisines with their displays of peacock pies and roast herons. France had established itself as a culinary superpower.

A principal theme in the story of food during the ensuing two centuries was the rapid spread of French fine cooking throughout Europe and its gradual percolation down the social scale. However, this is far from being the whole story, and despite the domination of French cuisine at higher levels, most nations managed to cling proudly to their own indigenous traditions. Hopefully this will be apparent in the recipes themselves in the sections that follow.

New Ingredients

Many new foods from the Americas, like maize, potatoes, tomatoes, capsicums, and squashes, started to arrive in Europe during the course of the sixteenth century. Some, like the turkey, were quickly adopted, but it took much longer for the potential of others to be realized. The Spanish and Portuguese, with their colonies in Central and South America, were the first to exploit many of these novel foods. Potatoes and tomatoes were particularly slow to be adopted by Europeans. Early botanists recognized them as belonging to a plant family with many poisonous members, and there was considerable resistance to their use as foods. Nowadays we associate the tomato with Italian pasta dishes, particularly those in the Neapolitan tradition, but these did not really appear on the scene until the nineteenth century. When the Spanish started to introduce the tomato into Naples toward the end of the seventeenth century, it was only featured in a handful of dishes. Even a hundred years later it was not being used as much in Neapolitan sauces as sour grapes or oranges.

Chocolate imported from Central America became a popular drink in Spain during the second half of the sixteenth century, but its use did not become widespread throughout Europe until a hundred years later. Although a few cacao-based sweetmeats appeared in the seventeenth century, chocolate confections did not become really significant until the nineteenth century. By the mid-seventeenth century, when chocolate drinking was making inroads into European courts, tea and coffee were also gaining immense importance as social beverages. However, they were expensive luxuries and it was a long time before they became available to all.

Although it was an Old World foodstuff known since classical antiquity, sugar became cheaper and much more widespread during the seventeenth and eighteenth centuries. This was due to the initiative of Portuguese and British planters who exploited the equable climate of their South American and Caribbean colonies to grow sugarcane in vast quantities. Consequently, the range of confections and preserves available to Europeans grew enormously during this period. Other discoveries in the Americas that proved significant to the confectioner were vanilla and pineapples. Vanilla, introduced into Naples by its Spanish ruling class, found its way into Neapolitan frozen desserts as early as the 1690s. Pineapples could not survive the long voyage across the Atlantic, so a few enthusiastic botanists explored methods of cultivating them in Europe. By the eighteenth century they were even being grown in chilly England in heated greenhouses.

The introduction of some New World species had surprising results. In the eighteenth century, chance pollination in a French garden between a strawberry species from Chile and another from Virginia resulted in a brand new large-fruited strawberry that became the ancestor of our modern varieties. However, it was not just chance that led to many new discoveries. More systematic approaches to understanding the natural world were being developed by botanists and horticulturalists. These would have a direct impact on the development of improved varieties of fruits and vegetables. An air of experimentation was everywhere. In Naples, even street vendors were becoming familiar with the newly discovered refrigerant properties of salt and ice mixtures and were developing the first European ices. On the outskirts of the same city, large workshops mass-producing dried pasta with large screw presses became Europe's first food factories.

KITCHENS AND CULINARY EQUIPMENT

There were many improvements in cooking facilities during this period. Roasting still took place in front of large fireplaces, but mechanical spit-turning mechanisms became much more commonplace and were even used in farmhouses. In England, with its rich coalfields, coal became the preferred cooking medium. It was cheap and enabled meats to be cooked to perfection in front of newly designed roasting ranges with raised fire baskets. These pushed out a much fiercer radiant heat than the old down-hearths, where wood was burnt at floor level. As a result the atmosphere of British towns became heavily polluted. But what did this matter, when the Englishman's table could be dressed with the finest roast meats to be found anywhere in Europe?

It was in the realm of fine cookery that the most important developments took place. The increasing use of the charcoal stewing stove enabled precise temperature control for the production of demanding sauces and cooking delicate foods like fish to perfection. These stoves were usually located at a good working height under large windows. This allowed optimum illumination and a means for the escape of noxious fumes. New flat-bottomed copper stewpans began to replace bronze pots with tripod legs, which were used for cooking over embers at ground level. Cauldrons hanging over smoky fires gave way more and more to purpose-built boilers with their own enclosed furnaces. As a result, cooking processes became cleaner and less backbreaking.

In substantial households, the area of the building designated for food preparation was a complex of purpose-built rooms. In addition to the kitchen, there were usually various larders for storage and a separate pastry room. In France, salads, confections, and other dessert foods were prepared in a separate suite of rooms called the *office*.

An English roasting range, c. 1817, with clockwork roasting mechanism. The screen in front of the fire not only reflects the intense heat of the coal fire back onto the meat, speeding up cooking time, but it also shields the cook and warms the dishes.

The *officier* (confectioner) who presided over this workshop was frequently the highest-paid culinary professional in the establishment. During the seventeenth and eighteenth centuries, the *officier's* role was completely separate from that of the *pâtissier* (pastry cook), who also worked in his own specific space. However, after the French Revolution, the two tasks became synonymous.

During the course of the eighteenth and nineteenth centuries, copper-smiths and iron founders provided both domestic and professional cooks with a remarkable new range of braising pans, saucepans, and sugar boilers. An almost infinite variety of copper, pewter, wooden, and ceramic molds also became available, enabling the creation of some of the most decorative dishes ever displayed on European tables.

THE TABLE SETTING

Dramatic changes also took place in the way in which food was presented and consumed at table. A spectacular new dining protocol emerged from Versailles and took other European courts by storm. This was *service à la Française* (table service in the French manner), which evolved from Italian

Renaissance methods of regulating the table. As in earlier periods, the food was set out in a series of buffet-like arrangements called courses. The chief innovations of *service à la Française* were in the first and final courses of the meal.

The first course of a dinner served in this way featured a choice of rich soups and stews called the *grosses entrées.* By the early eighteenth century these were being served in spectacular new vessels called tureens, made of silver or silver gilt. After the soups and stews had been served, the tureens were removed from the table, leaving what were considered to be unsightly empty spaces. These voids were immediately filled with other substantial fish and meat dishes called *relevés*—known as *removes* in English. Other important dishes presented in the first course were the *roti*—roast—and the *hors d'oeuvres*, which were not little starters like today, but smaller dishes scattered symmetrically between the *grosses entrées.* The second course of the meal usually consisted of an array of less substantial meat and fish dishes and included both savory and sweet *entremets*—vegetable dishes and sweet pastries.

The final course was called *le fruit*—the fruit—or *le dessert.* This was derived from the *issue de la table* of the medieval period, when the sovereign was given sweetmeats and spiced wine for his digestion. It was a spectacular finale to the meal, containing sumptuous arrangements of fruit, confections, cookies, and ices. In the seventeenth century it was fashionable to arrange the dessert foods in high pyramids on ascending salvers. By the middle of the eighteenth century it was often laid out as a tabletop formal garden, complete with sugar sculpture and porcelain figures. In seventeenth-century Italy, high-status tables were often graced with spectacular sugar sculptures called *trionfi*—triumphs. These usually had emblematic or symbolic meanings. One of a number presented at a feast in Rome in 1686 in honor of James II of England was in the form of Neptune, referring to the King's role as Admiral of the Fleet.

Sugar sculpture, or trionfo, *of Neptune for a feast in Rome in 1686.*

Although *service à la Française* created a great spectacle, it had its drawbacks, one being that many dishes on the table became cold while the guests were eating their soup. To correct this, a new pattern of dining emerged in the early decades of the nineteenth century and became known as *service à la Russe*—service in the Russian style.

Allegedly introduced into Paris by a Russian prince called Alexander Kurakin, this involved serving the individual dishes of the meal sequentially—that is one at a time, rather like we do nowadays. This new procedure of service was slow to catch on, but by the end of the nineteenth century it eventually displaced *service à la Française.*

SALADS

Instructions for making salads are rather sparse in seventeenth- and eighteenth-century French cookbooks. There are only three in La Varenne's *Le cuisinier François* (1651), the most important cookbook of its time. However, during this period, salads were not the responsibility of the cook and were rarely made in the kitchen. They were assembled in the *office*, or confectionery, far from the overbearing heat of the great roasting fires and stoves, which could easily wither the freshly picked greens and herbs. This is why the most complete collection of salad recipes from this early period is in a little book on confections rather than cooking called *Le confiturier royal*, published in 1662. As well as a range of salad recipes suitable for the different seasons of the year, it contains detailed instructions for making an elaborate salad in the form of a royal crown (see recipe 166).[2]

On the whole the French had a preference for very simple salads made from one main vegetable, rather than fussy mixtures of ingredients. Pierre de Lune, cook to the Duke of Rohan, provided the following list of salads popular in the middle of the seventeenth century.

Pomegranate Salad	Salad of Cresses
Lemon Salad	Purslane Salad
Salad of Bigarade Oranges	Lettuce Salad
Caper Salad	Salad of Macedonian Parsley
Salad of Portugal Oranges	Hop Salad
Salad of Cucumbers in Vinegar	Salad of Sugared Capers
Asparagus Salad	Radish Salad

In the Italian peninsula, salads were frequently made from the succulent young tendrils of pumpkin plants, vines, and other young shoots. Flowers were also popular—borage, bugloss, rosemary, and elder blossoms were all dressed with oil, vinegar, salt, and a little sugar. In Naples, jasmine flowers bathed in morning dew were dressed in this way to make a perfumed salad of "the finest quality."[3] More complex salads were based on a foundation of bread or biscuit soaked in wine or vinegar and topped with a variety of salad greens, olives, and salt fish like anchovies and *tarantello*—preserved tuna. These so-called "Royal Salads" were also popular in Spain and Austria.

Though both simple and mixed salads had been popular in Britain since the Tudor period, the second half of the seventeenth century saw the publication of many recipes for flamboyant and highly decorative Grand Salads, which were usually the first dishes to be delivered to the table. Despite contemporary reports from foreign travelers that the British ate very few vegetables, there are actually more recipes for salads in the English cookbooks of this period than those of any other nation.

Soups

At upper-class tables, soups or pottages were consumed as a prelude to other dishes. In poorer households, the soup was often the only dish of the meal. They varied considerably from country to country, but in most European kitchens they were made by cooking meat, fish, or vegetables in a stock, or broth, which was then poured over pieces of bread. This bread was sometimes fried or toasted and was known as *sops*—thus *soup* and also the name for the meal *supper*. In seventeenth-century Italy a soup could be served over dried, crisp bread or even sponge biscuits. Cold soups called *gazpachos* were popular in southern Spain. These were made by pounding the bread with oil, vinegar, garlic, and anchovies (see recipe 21).

In France, an elaborate soup was made by pouring the broth over *profiteroles*—hollowed-out bread rolls filled with a savory stuffing (see recipe 157). Sometimes little fried or baked pastries were used to garnish the rims of soup plates (see recipe 18). Before the soup tureen came into use at the end of the seventeenth century, it was common to bake a ring of puff pastry on the rim of a large plate or charger before pouring the soup into the plate. The pastry collar prevented the soup from leaking out over the table. Soup plate margins were sometimes ornamented with elaborate garnishes cut from different colored vegetables. It was also common for the surface of a soup to be toasted with a red-hot fire shovel or a special tool called a salamander. This created an attractive caramelized skin upon which garnishes of pomegranate seeds and pistachios could be floated.

In Spain and France, the liquid in which meat and vegetables were cooked was often served as a soup, followed by the meat and vegetables as separate courses. A celebrated mixed-meat stew of this kind made with garbanzos and root vegetables was the *olla podrida,* or *olio* (see recipe 29).

During the early nineteenth century, very light but well-flavored clear soups or *consommés* became fashionable. These were made with clarified stock and often contained little pieces of vegetable cut into fancy shapes. Savory custards made of seasoned cream and egg were also stamped out into little shapes with ornamental cutters and used to embellish these clear soups.

Meat, Poultry, and Game

Because there were no freezers or refrigerators, fresh meat could not be stored for very long. As a result, much that was surplus to immediate requirements was preserved by salting, smoking, collaring, and pickling. These activities were not usually carried out by the cook, as kitchens were too hot for these processes. However, preserved meats of various kinds were used as essential ingredients in many dishes. Slices of ham and bacon were often cooked with the other meats and vegetables in the early stages of preparing soups, stews, and sauces. An intensely flavored coulis called essence of ham was used to give extra relish to stews and sauces. Smoked and preserved sausages of all kinds were also added to various dishes for extra interest.

Of all the fresh butcher's meats, the most revered for fine cooking was veal. It was admired both for its delicate flavor and light color. However, many cuts of veal were rather dry, so a process called larding was used to ensure that it remained succulent. This was carried out by sewing little strips of bacon fat into the meat with a special needle called a larding pin. The strips of fat, or lardoons, were often rolled in herbs and spices before they were sewn into the meat. Larding was a very skilful technique and required a great deal of practice. A well larded *fricandeau* of veal or fillet of beef was as admired for its visual beauty as for its flavor. Hare, venison, and game birds were all frequently larded. Suckling pig and other young animals, particularly juvenile geese, were never larded as they carried their own stores of fat. Some diners did not like larded meat, so both larded and unlarded were often on offer (see recipe 26). Sometimes citrus peels, such as orange and citron, were cut into strips and sewn into joints of meat and poultry. On some occasions candied peel lardoons were even decorated with gold and silver leaf (see p. 13).

During the medieval and Renaissance periods a very large variety of wild fowl was consumed. Peacocks, herons, cranes, swans, and small songbirds were all eaten with relish. As the seventeenth century advanced many of these large showy birds became unfashionable. However, small songbirds like thrushes, ortolans, and larks retained their popularity. Of the game birds, the partridge was considered the most worthy of the prince's table and was prized throughout Europe.

Of all domestic fowl, the capon or castrated cockerel was the most esteemed. Its large brawny breasts were the foundation of countless dishes. Pigeons and doves were also bred for the table in prodigious quantities. In France, aristocratic landowners housed enormous colonies of these birds in dovecotes. They were very unpopular with local villagers, because the pigeons often destroyed their crops.

FISH

In Catholic and some Protestant nations, the strict dietary rules regarding the consumption of meat during Lent, Advent, and on Fridays continued to be applied in much the same way as in earlier centuries. As a result, fish was an immensely important part of most people's diet. Even a cursory glance through the cookbooks will reveal that many more fish species found their way into the kitchen than in modern Europe. People who lived in landlocked regions remote from the sea had to depend on what their lakes, rivers, and ponds could provide. Easily farmed fish like carp were therefore very important. In these inland areas another option was preserved fish like salt cod, which could be bought in from the coast. Oysters kept alive in little barrels were also consumed in vast quantities, often hundreds of miles from the ocean.

Less popular in Europe today, but highly esteemed during this period in most countries, was the freshwater predator, the pike. This was a favorite of the celebrated British angler Isaac Walton, who gives a detailed recipe for roasting it on a spit (see recipe 39). In Italy, pike was larded with strips of eel flesh and served with a sauce of capers, shrimps, and rose vinegar.[4] Rivers like the Rhine, Thames, and Seine were much less polluted than in modern times and salmon could often be caught where the rivers flowed through large cities. Sturgeon was another large fish that frequently swam into estuaries and was highly esteemed everywhere. It was frequently pickled or made into pies.

Countries bordering the cold waters of the North Sea and the Baltic consumed vast quantities of herring and its smaller relatives, sprats and smelt. These were salted, smoked, and pickled in an infinite number of ways. In Mediterranean countries, tuna, swordfish, mullet, squid, and octopus were consumed by everybody. Preserved fish like anchovies were also of great importance. *Botargo*, salted mullet roe, and *tarantella*, salted tuna belly, were produced in southern Italy but esteemed elsewhere as delicacies.

As will be seen from a few recipes in this book, fish were frequently combined with meat in unusual ways (see notes on recipe 65). Eel was sometimes cooked with pork, while anchovies and oysters were very popular in beef and mutton dishes. A classic combination in nineteenth-century high-class French food was lobster or crayfish butter with chicken (recipe 171).

VEGETABLES AND FUNGI

Like fish, vegetables were an important part of the meager diet on days when flesh was prohibited. This may be the reason why vegetable cooking became much more developed in countries where these dietary rules were strictly applied, such as Catholic Spain, Italy, and France. When the Church stipulated that its communicants should be vegetarians for a large part of the year, it made sense to cook vegetables in more exciting ways.

The poor relied a great deal on cabbages, dried legumes, and root vegetables like turnips to get them through the dark days of winter. Potatoes did not become a significant feature of a subsistence diet on the European mainland until the nineteenth century, although they had become well established in Ireland and northern England by the previous century. The wealthy encouraged their gardeners to grow large crops of fresh peas, asparagus, artichokes, cardoons, and salsify. In early-nineteenth-century haute cuisine, vegetables were exploited in ingenious ways for decorative effect. Spectacular side dishes called *chartreuses* were ornamented with lozenges and geometric shapes cut out of slices of vegetables of contrasting colors (see recipe 162). Tiny stars, lozenges, and turned balls of carrot, turnip, and other root vegetables were used to garnish consommé.

Among the fungi, truffles and morels were the most valued in the kitchen. Both were major ingredients in French and Italian high-class cooking. *Mousserons*, or fairy ring mushrooms (*Marasmius oreades*), were also popular in France, where they were dressed in a cream sauce and served on fried bread croutons. Field mushrooms were cooked in an enormous number of ways. One outstanding French court recipe from the eighteenth century involved deep-frying them in puff pastry (see recipe 120). The same source recommended a strong seasoning made by drying mushrooms, morels, and truffles in the sun and reducing them to a fine powder. This was used to season the bacon fat used for larding meat and game.

SAUCES

French sauce recipes published at the beginning of this period were entirely medieval in character and few in number. Most had been around for centuries and were based on vinegar, sugar, and spices. There were far more on offer in the Italian and even the English culinary traditions, though these too tended to be largely sweet and sour in nature and heavily spiced. In Italy there were two kinds—*sapore* (relishes) and *salse* (sauces). Examples of both kinds can be found in the first and second recipe sections of this book. The English master cook Robert May, in his *The Accomplisht Cook* (1660), categorized sauces according to the type of meat or fish for which they were intended, as in the box here.

✣ SEVERAL SAUCES FOR ROAST CHICKENS

1. Gravy, and the juice or slices of orange.
2. Butter, verjuice, and gravy of the chicken, or mutton gravy.

> 3. Butter and vinegar boil'd together, put to it a little sugar, then make thin sops of bread, lay the roast chicken on them, and serve them up hot.
> 4. Take sorrel, wash and stamp it, then have thin slices of manchet, put them in a dish with some vinegar, strained sorrel, sugar, some gravy, beaten cinnamon, beaten butter, and some slices of orange or lemon, and strew thereon some cinnamon and sugar.
> 5. Take slic't oranges, and put to them a little white wine, rose-water, beaten mace, ginger, some sugar, and butter, set them on a chafing dish of coals and stew them; then have some likes of manchet round the dish finely carved and lay the chickens roasted on the sauce.[5]

After the introduction of roux and coulis in the 1660s, French cooks started to rapidly develop a new range of sauces, including classics like béchamel, ravigotte, and mayonnaise. By 1755, there were over 70 sauces listed in *Les soupers de la cour*, nearly all of them new. In 1846, Queen Victoria's chef Francatelli gives recipes for 105 sauces.

PASTRIES

Success in pastry depends very much on precise proportions, delicate handling, and cool working conditions. Temperature control and timing are also crucial at the baking stage. In most early modern cookbooks, pastry recipes are often vague and it is difficult to get good results by following such sketchy instructions. This does not mean that excellent pastry was not being made—just that the descriptive language of recipes had not developed enough to reflect actual practice. This changed in 1653 with the publication of

Le pastissier François, a book doubtfully attributed to François Pierre La Varenne. Its recipes, written with tremendous clarity and an almost scientific precision, are unprecedented.

If the pastry cooks of France were developing a rational approach to creating the perfect, melt-in-the-mouth pastry, those of other nations were more concerned with exploiting the artistic potential of the medium. Since the medieval period, pastry cases had been enlivened with applied decorations and in some cases even gilded. Birds in their full plumage were frequently placed on top as a visual clue to a pie's contents. The earliest European printed designs for decorative pastry appeared in 1660 in *The Accomplisht Cook* by Robert May.

Austrian pie design, 1719.

These crude woodcuts reveal a vanished world of sinuously shaped custard pies arranged like knot gardens, multicolored tarts resembling stained glass windows, and mince pies forming intricate kaleidoscope patterns on the plate. About 60 years later, a London pastry teacher called Edward Kidder published some even more remarkable designs. These show in detail how to embellish a lamb pasty with a bird perched in a tree or a venison pasty with a magnificent pastry stag.[6]

In 1719, Conrad Hagger, master cook to the Archbishop of Salzburg, illustrated his *Neues saltzburgisches koch-buch* with a large number of highly detailed plates of fine pastry work. These designs afford the best clue we have to the appearance of the food of this period.

✈ NEAPOLITAN TRIONFI FROM 1692

Suggestions For Edible Table Decorations

1. A pie in the form of a gilded dragon that breathes perfumed smoke from its mouth.
2. A carriage made of royal pastry filled with white comfits, driven by a cupid and pulled by two white doves.
3. A carriage pulled by two sea dolphins, driven by Neptune with two sea nymphs.
4. A castle of sugar, encircled with artillery, bombardiers and soldiers.
5. An ostrich folded from a napkin, or beautifully made of sugar paste.
6. Trajan's Arch in Rome made of sugar paste.
7. An obelisk made of gelatin with little fishes of divers colors inside, all within a sugar coronet flecked with gold.
8. A turkey roasted, larded with lardoons of candied citron, with the points adorned, some with gold, some with silver, with wings, neck and tail made of sugar paste all embellished with gold.
9. A pie in the form of a suckling pig, adorned with gold on its skin, with a chain around its neck of gilded sugar, with slices of eggs arranged round the middle.
10. A royal eagle with two heads, made of puff pastry, filled with marzipan paste and Genoese quince paste.
11. Obelisks made of ice and filled with fruit of every sort.
12. A hunter with dogs on leashes, all made of butter.[7]

There are pastries made in the form of dolphins, pies surmounted with pastry animals, and a multiplicity of magnificent tarts, marzipans, and cakes. This ornamental pastry tradition was carried into the nineteenth century, when Antonin Carême's *Le pâtissier pittoresque* was published in Paris in 1815. Carême wedded the decorative skills of the confectioner to those of the pastry cook to produce architectural fantasies called *pièces montées*.

A metate and roller for grinding chocolate.

A French dessert table, 1751.

These were usually made out of an inedible pastry called *pâte d'office* and decorated with spun sugar, nougat, and sugar paste. As well as acting as table centerpieces, they doubled as cake stands and were usually garnished with displays of little pastries.

DESSERTS

During the course of the seventeenth century, a greater understanding of the properties of sugar led to a dramatic increase in the range of confectionery and sweet foods. This trend continued into succeeding centuries, but with ever-growing supplies of sugar, these luxury foods, once confined to the very wealthy, became available to most social groups. Professional confectionery shops sold a bewildering array of comfits, biscuits, candies, marmalades, and fruit preserves. By the eighteenth century, these establishments were adding alcoholic liqueurs and ices to their wares. At the right price, they would also provide the table ornaments and sugar sculptures necessary to dress a high-class dessert table in the most fashionable mode.

Chocolate, both for drinking and cooking, was sold by confectioners in the form of small tablets. They processed the raw cacao beans by roasting them to remove the skins and then ground them on a *metate*, a concave stone slab heated by a chafing dish of charcoal. This procedure melted the cocoa butter in the beans and the grinding process pulverized the solids, blending the two together into chocolate. Sugar and other ingredients, such as cinnamon, were then added. The earliest chocolate sweets date from the 1660s. They were called Nuts of Toulon, or the Queen's Chocolados, and

---

✦ AN ITALIAN DESSERT COURSE 1662

Second service from the Credenza

A peach tart	Muscat grapes
Honeyed cream in wafers	Damascus prunes
Creamy ricotta	Pears of every sort

Sheep's cheese	Lazerole medlers
Cheese from Lodi	Peaches
Marzolino cheese	Apricots
Black cherry supa	Peach kernels
Peeled fennel stems	Cherries of every sort

Third service from the Credenza

Wash and prepare the fruit, serve the confectionery in regal dishes

A dish of candied black cherries	A dish of candied pumpkin
A dish of candied lettuce stems	A dish of both sweet and hot mostaccioli
Four dishes of white comfits	A dish of conserve of jasmine, violet
A dish of peach paste	and lemon flowers
A dish of candied citron	A dish of Genoa paste[8]

were made by candying immature cacao beans. Various chocolate marzipans and chocolate pastilles were described in the confectioners' recipe books published in the eighteenth century. However, the earliest true chocolates seem to have emerged from Naples, where they were appropriately called *diavolini*—little devils (see recipe 147).

ICES

During the sixteenth century, various alchemical authors noted that when salt was added to ice, it resulted in a refrigerant effect that could cause liquids to freeze. However, it was not until the second half of the seventeenth century that this process was exploited for making sorbets and ice creams. The equipment required was cheap and the freezing process elegantly simple. A pewter pot known as a *sorbetière* was allowed to cool in a wooden pail packed full of ice and salt. The mixture to be frozen was put into the *sorbetière* and stirred with a spatula. As the mixture froze to the sides of the vessel it was scraped down with the blade of the spatula. If continuously stirred, it was discovered that flavored syrups would freeze into a pleasantly smooth *sorbetto* (water ice), from the Arabic *sharāb*, meaning syrup (or wine). The trick was to make sure that the concentration of sugar in the syrup was exactly right—too much and it would not freeze properly, too little and it turned into unpleasant hard ice crystals.

Naples was instrumental in the development of this exciting new delicacy. By the late 1600s, an extraordinary range of *sorbetti* was being made for sale by professional vendors in the city. Chocolate and vanilla flavors were both established at least as early as the 1690s and a range of less-familiar ices made with grape must, pine nut comfits, and candied pumpkin were also on offer. Francesco Procopio, a Sicilian who opened the famous Café Procope in Paris in 1686, is credited with spreading the craze to France. Procopio and his fellow professionals seem to have kept rather quiet about their secrets. Recipes for ices in cookbooks from this early period appear to be based on guesswork, rather than a true working knowledge of the process. Nevertheless, it was not long before the French mastered the art. In 1768, the first book exclusively devoted to the subject of making ices was published in Paris.[9] Among the numerous flavors it enumerates are cream of chestnut, saffron mousse, white coffee, and a variety of ices based on liqueurs and wines, like cream of Barbados and Tokay.

At this period ices were frequently molded into novelty shapes like fruits, animals, and even cuts of meat. Ice creams were also used as fillings for cakes and tarts (see recipe 141). During the early nineteenth century elaborate molded ice cream puddings and bombes started to emerge. One of the earliest was an iced cabinet pudding invented by Antonin Carême. This famous *pâtissier* had worked for the English heir to the throne and was familiar with the popular British cabinet pudding, a steamed custard pudding designed for using up stale slices of bread. He transformed this commonplace dish by sandwiching layers of sponge cake soaked with maraschino liqueur between pineapple ice cream and scatterings of preserved peel.

DRINKS

One of the most important developments in the social history of this period was the gradual adoption of tea, coffee, and chocolate. At first there was considerable resistance from conservative wine and beer drinkers to these exotic beverages. As a result some early promoters resorted to claiming powerful aphrodisiac properties for all three drinks to encourage the public to try them. However, once they were established at court, their usage gradually spread down the social scale. At first, oriental porcelain was used for the service of these drinks, but as the eighteenth century advanced, newly established European porcelain manufactories started to produce their own designs for the necessary equipage. Cafés and teahouses became a new and socially important feature of most European cities. All three beverages were enthusiastically adopted by both cooks and confectioners as flavorings. Chocolate tarts, tea creams, and coffee wafers and ices soon appeared on the scene. In François Massialot's *Le cuisinier royal et bourgeois* (Paris, 1691), there was even a meat recipe in the Central American style that included chocolate, though this does not seem to have caught on.[10]

As distillation techniques developed, more and more powerful cordials and *ratafias* (see recipe 98) became available during this period. These pungent spirits were the precursors of our modern liqueurs and were made with fruit, herb, or spice flavorings. Many had romantic names like *perfetto amore, rosolio,* and *usquebaugh* (see recipe 100).

A NOTE ON THE RECIPES

Many of the recipes in this book are translated into English for the first time. Some of those originally in English are from previously unpublished manuscript sources or from rare printed books that are not generally available. Archaic spellings have been retained in the English recipes. None have been adapted for the modern kitchen, though difficult terms and procedures are explained in the accompanying narrative. There are recipes from France, Italy, Spain, Portugal, Germany, Austria, Holland, Scotland, and England. Because of the domination of European cuisine by France during this period, it is natural that French recipes should outnumber those of the other countries. And since there were more recipe books published in England than any other European nation, English recipes come a close second.

The interpretation of old recipes is fraught with difficulties, particularly when it comes to the subject of weights and measures. In Europe at this period, not only did these units vary from country to country, but they often had completely different meanings from one city to another. For instance, a Spanish unit of weight called the *libro* was roughly equivalent to 400 grams in Barcelona, but only 372 grams in Pamplona. In Portugal, a liquid measure known as a *canada* was about 2.4 liters in Oporto, but only 1.6 in Lisbon. In one 1829 Milanese recipe, we are directed to grate 2 *soldi* of bread. A *soldo* was a low-denomination coin, equivalent to a cent or a penny. What the author is telling us is to grate two cents worth of bread. This creates a serious difficulty for a modern cook, who will wonder just how much bread could be bought in Milan in 1829 for this sum. Wherever possible these obscure measurements are explained and clarified in the recipe notes.

COOKING PERIOD FOOD TODAY

All of the dishes in this book could be prepared using modern kitchen equipment. However, if you are adventurous and want to get a little closer to our ancestors' experience of kitchen work, you would probably like to try some of their cooking methods for yourself. Before you attempt this, it would be advisable to visit an historic site where hearth cookery and other traditional methods are demonstrated by experts.

Some old techniques are more feasible than others. Not many modern American homes have an open fireplace suitable for spit roasting or cauldron cooking, but many have a backyard and a barbecue area that can be adapted with a little imagination. Clockwork spit mechanisms are now easily purchased online and setting one up to use in your backyard is not difficult (see appendix). Dutch oven cooking is still popular, and this age-old technique is identical to the braising and daubing methods used in many of the recipes in this book. Dutch ovens and tripod cooking pots are great for using over campfires. Baking food by wrapping it in wet paper and covering it with hot embers (recipes 22 and 88) is also easily achieved in this context. An excellent introduction to this type of cooking is William Rubel's book *The Magic of Fire* (2004).

Building a wood-fired oven for baking might seem like an ambitious venture, but it would make an excellent and rewarding school or community project. There is now a growing literature on do-it-yourself oven construction, so there is no end of advice on this subject. When it comes to decorative dishes like molded ices and gelatins, it is actually possible nowadays to buy original nineteenth- and early-twentieth-century equipment and molds from online auction sites at bargain prices. The old-fashioned cranked ice cream machines that use ice and salt are still available and are very close to the kind of equipment that was used for making ices in the nineteenth century. Failing one of these, a tall stainless steel container with a lid, surrounded with an ice and salt mixture in a bucket, is an excellent substitute for a *sorbetière*. Scrape the ice down as it freezes with a wooden spatula or spoon.

2

❧ THE BAROQUE AND ROCOCO ERA, 1650–1750

The period covered in this section was one of the most important in the development of European cuisine. It was in many ways a culinary equivalent of the intellectual enlightenment that unfolded at the same time. However, this was an era of gradual development, rather than one of overnight change, and many of the food traditions of earlier centuries continued to flourish alongside new innovations.

The aftermath of the Thirty Years War (1618–1648) saw the emergence of a methodical new style of fine cookery in France with a systematic approach to basic mixtures, ingredients, and techniques. This innovative gastronomic style saw its first expression in a handful of books published in Paris during the 1650s. The most influential of these was *Le cuisinier François* (1653) by François Pierre La Varenne. Like many other cooks of his generation, La Varenne had served as a military cook in the service of an aristocratic commander. It was during the prolonged period of warfare between 1636 and 1648 that French cooks appear to have transformed a style of cookery that had not changed radically since the medieval period. Through necessity, they used a smaller range of spices and kitchen processes were simplified and codified for maximum efficiency in the field. This trimmed-down gastronomic model eventually transformed high-class cookery throughout Europe.

Nicholas de Bonnefons, one of La Varenne's contemporaries and the author of *Les delices de la campagne* (1654), advocated a culinary style based on simplicity: "A cabbage soup should taste entirely of cabbage; a leek soup of leeks; a turnip soup of turnips."[1] He ridiculed "depraved ragoûts" that contained a multiplicity of hashes, mushrooms, and spices and recommended a cuisine based on diversity and clean flavors. The third important French author of this decade, Pierre de Lune, in his *Le nouveau cuisinier* (1656), methodically lists the basic ingredients that should always be at hand in an efficiently run kitchen, including the *paquet*—a bundle of bacon, chives, thyme, cloves, chervil, and parsley—an essential kitchen requisite that would later evolve into the *bouquet garni*.

During this period in England, the population was recovering from the huge upheavals of the Civil War (1642–1651) and becoming disenchanted with the austerity of the Puritan administration that had governed the country until 1660. The bestselling cookbooks published in the 1650s and 1660s tended to look nostalgically back to the grand hospitality and lavish food of the pre–Civil War period. It is often said that British food at this period was backward and still strongly medieval in character, but this analysis is belied by the appearance of Robert May's *The Accomplisht Cook* in 1660. This extraordinary book is in many ways as innovative as La Varenne's and in some areas of cookery is even more sophisticated. His section on sauces is much more extensive than that of any French book of this period and he has far more to say on the subject of salads. His book also contains invaluable images of food, particularly of the elaborate pastry work of the period. England was also to produce Europe's earliest female cookbook author, the prolific Hannah Wooley, who ran a cooking school in the East End of London in the 1660s.

Like their French and English contemporaries, the cookbook writers of the Italian peninsula in the second half of the seventeenth century tended to instruct their readers in a sophisticated aristocratic style of cookery. In 1662, Bartolomeo Stefani, cook to the Gonzaga family in Modena, issued a small book of rather old-fashioned recipes, which indicates that food at least in some parts of Italy had not changed a great deal since the previous century. In the 1690s, Antonio Latini offered one of the best insights into the cuisine of baroque Naples in his monumental two-volume *Lo scalco alla moderna* (1692 and 1694). Here are the earliest recipes for tomatoes and chilies in any Italian cookbook. He also briefly touches on that other Neapolitan specialty, the frozen dessert.

In the Netherlands, a few cookbooks emerged from the printing presses of Amsterdam, including early editions of La Varenne and other French authors. The anonymous *De verstandige kock* (1669), the only native Dutch recipe book of the period, gives insight into the unpretentious food of the merchant class at this period, though it does contain a number of foreign dishes. In the German-speaking parts of Europe, large encyclopedic cookbooks were popular. The most important of these was Conrad Hagger's *Neues saltzburgisches koch-buch* (1719), the most profusely illustrated cookbook of the early modern period.

French cookbooks of the later seventeenth and early eighteenth century, such as those of François Massialot (1682) and Vincent La Chapelle (1736), abandoned the simplicity advocated by La Varenne and de Bonnefons and promoted an extravagant style of cookery that had its origins at the court of Louis XIV. With its lavish use of coulis, a highly flavored meat concentrate, and rich stews, bisques, and ragoûts, this was cooking at its most extravagant. From the 1730s onward there was a strong reaction against this profligate cuisine and a simpler approach to cookery started to emerge, which is described in the works of François Marin (1739) and Menon (1747). During this period French cooking had a profound effect on high-status dining in most other European countries and French cooks were often to be found running the kitchens of the aristocracy and the wealthy.

Salads and Cold Dishes

1. SALAD OF POMEGRANATE

France 1651. (La Varenne, 124)

Pick your pomegranate seeds, put them on a plate. Sugar them and garnish with lemon slices and serve.

Nothing could be simpler and more refreshing than this appetizing assemblage of garnet colored pomegranate kernels. To extract the seeds with ease, make vertical scores like lines of longitude all around the fruit with a sharp knife and then remove the skin. Pull the fruit apart and put it in a bowl of water. The bitter yellow pith will float and can easily be discarded; the seeds sink to the bottom and can be put in a sieve to drain. If you want to make your salad look really authentic, notch the rind of the lemon slices so they look like cogwheels. Arrange them as a garnish around the rim of your plate.

2. TO GARNISH BRAWN OR PIG BRAWN

England 1660. (May, 194)

Leach your brawn, and dish it on a plate in a fair clean dish, then put a rosemary branch on the top being first dipped in the white of an egg well beaten to a froth, or wet in water and sprinkled with flour, or a sprig of rosemary gilt with gold; the brawn spotted also with gold and silver leaves, or let your sprig be of a straight sprig of yew tree, or a straight furze bush and put about the brawn stuck round with bay-leaves three ranks round, and spotted with red and yellow jelly about the dish sides, also the same jelly and some of the brawn leached, jagged, or cut with tin moulds, and carved lemons, oranges and barberries, bay-leaves gilt, red beets, pickled barberries, pickled gooseberries, or pickled grapes.

Carved fruits for garnishing.

This spectacular English special-occasion dish was also garnished with elaborately carved citrus fruits. Brawn was a kind of pickled pork prepared from domestic boar meat poached until very tender in a souse of wine, vinegar, and spices. The cuts of boned meat, which were called *collars*, were cooked for such a long time that they were tightly wrapped in linen parcels to stop them disintegrating. When they cooled, they became firmer as a result of the jelly released in the cooking process. Collars of brawn could be kept for a number of weeks in the souse. To *leach* the brawn was to carve it into thin slices. This now-extinct dish had been a mainstay of English cooking since the late medieval period when it was usually served with mustard at the beginning of a meal.

At important feasts it was presented to table in a highly decorative form, often gilded with gold leaf and decorated with colored jellies. One of the side products of making brawn was a lot of highly flavored savory jelly, which was often colored red with cochineal and yellow with saffron, stamped into decorative slices, and used as a garnish.

If you want to replicate this extraordinary dish, cover a nice cut of pork tenderloin and two pig's trotters in a large saucepan with half water, half dry white wine. Add a few tablespoons of vinegar, some salt, pepper, whole mace, and a couple of bay leaves. Poach gently with the lid of the saucepan on until the tenderloin is cooked. Remove both the tenderloin and trotters. Strain the liquid through a fine strainer or jelly bag and divide it into two equal portions. Color one with saffron and the other with cochineal. Pour it into two soup bowls and put in a cool place to set into the colored jellies. Put half an apple in the middle of a large dish and insert a tall, straight rosemary sprig into it. When the tenderloin is really cold, cut it into thin slices and cover the middle of the dish with them, including the half apple, which should not be visible. Decorate the meat with small spots of edible gold and silver leaf and bay leaves. Try your hand at carving whole oranges. Put a circle of them round your brawn. Then cut the colored jellies into cubes and garnish the brim of your dish with them.

❧ 3. A GRAND SALAD ❧

England 1660. (May, 159)

Dish first round the centre slic'd figs, then currants, capers, almonds and raisins together; next beyond that, olives, beets, cabbidge-lettice, cucumbers, or slic't lemon carved; then oyl and vinegar beaten together, the best oyl you can get, and sugar or none, as you please; garnish the brims of the dish with orangado, slict lemon jagged, olives stuck with slic't almonds, sugar or none.

This attractive and colorful salad would have been dressed in a large glazed ceramic dish, as metal dishes were corroded by acids such as vinegar and lemon juice. John Evelyn, the English diarist warned,

That the *saladiere*, (Sallet–Dishes) be of Porcelane, or of the Holland-Delftware; neither too deep nor shallow, according to the quantity of the Sallet-Ingredients; Pewter, or even silver, not at all so well agreeing with Oyl and Vinegar, which leave their several Tinctures.[2]

The ingredients were chopped fine and arranged in concentric circles, rather like a target. The *orangado* used for garnishing the brims of the dishes were strips of orange peel preserved in syrup. The carved lemon slices were also called "jagged lemons," indicating that the rinds of the slices were cut with indentations. Other, more ambitious grand salads were often ornamented with a tall sprig of rosemary hung with red currants or other berries, a decoration known as a standard. One grand salad mentioned by May's contemporary William Rabisha was ornamented with a rock outcrop carved out of butter.[3]

☙ 4. TO MAKE A SALAD OF ARTICHOKES ❧

Netherlands 1669. (De verstandige kock, 5)

Take some artichokes, take off the leaves and make sure that no dirt is left on the bottoms (hearts). Then cut these and eat them with pepper, salt, sugar, oil and vinegar.

It seems strange to us today that sugar would be used in a salad of artichokes. However, it is still an important ingredient of many modern salad dressings, used to mollify the acidity of the vinegar. Artichokes were one of the major luxury vegetables of the early modern period and were often prepared in quite complicated ways. This simple Dutch salad is a straightforward and excellent way of serving this wonderful vegetable.

☙ 5. ROYAL SALAD ❧

Italy (Kingdom of Naples) 1694. (Latini, vol. 2, 150)

Take endive, or wild chicory, mince it finely and put it to one side, until you have prepared a large basin, at the bottom of which are eight, or ten biscottini, friselle, or taralli, soaked in water, and vinegar, with a little white salt; put the said chopped endive on top, intermix with other salad stuff, albeit minced finely, make the body of the said salad on top at your discretion, intermix with radishes cut into pieces lengthways, filling in the gaps in the said basin with the ingredients listed below, all arranged in order. Pinenuts four ounces; stoned olives six ounce; capers four ounce; one pomegranate; white and black grapes ten ounces; twelve anchovies; tarantello (salted belly of tuna) four ounces; botargo three ounces; comfits six ounces; preserved citron and preserved pumpkin twelve ounces; four hard boiled eggs; whole pistachios four ounces; four ounces of raisins; other black olives six ounces. Caviar, four ounces; minced flesh of white fish, six ounces; little radishes, salt, oil, and vinegar to taste, garnish the plate with slices of citrons, and citron flowers round about in order, take heed not to add salt or seasonings, until it goes to the table, and is about to be eaten.

This is a Southern ancestor of the well-known modern Tuscan bread salad. *Biscottini,* or "little biscuits," are in this case ship's biscuits, a hard dry rusk made by cutting bread into slices and putting it in the oven a second time to dry. *Friselle* and *taralli* are hard ring-shaped breads that are both still made in southern Italy. Like *biscottini* they were usually softened in water. The radishes of this period were white and long-rooted rather than the round, bright red ones popular today. *Tarantello* was a common ingredient in Italian recipes of the early modern period. It was made by salting part of the belly of young tuna fish. The city of Taranto was the center of production, but this ancient delicacy is no longer made in Italy. *Botargo,* a salty delicacy made of preserved fish roes, however, is still available, the most prized being made by salting tuna roe. Citrons or *cedri* were commonly grown in southern Italy and both the preserved peel and fresh flowers were popular ingredients in both sweet and savory dishes. Fresh lemon or orange flowers would make a good substitute. To make up for the lack of *tarantello,* a few extra anchovies could be used. Sugared comfits were a common garnish for dishes of this kind, those of anise or fennel being the most popular.

✦ OF GROCERIES, WINES, AND CHEESES OR OF THE SEASONINGS IN GENERAL

The ingredients used in the kitchen are:

Salt and saltpeter occasionally
Pepper, long pepper
Cloves
Nutmeg
Nutmeg flowers
Ginger
Mace
Sweet Almonds
Bitter Almonds
Pistachios

Currants
Coriander
Saffron

Spices

Cinnamon
Aniseed and juniper
Lemon
Orange
Pomegranate
Verjuice
Mustard, etc.

Wines And Liqueurs

The wines and liqueurs are:

The red vinegar and the white vinegar, or distilled
The very fine oil
The red wine
The Champagne wine made and the same wine, very green
The Rhine wine, etc.

Cheeses

The cheeses are:

The Parmesan
The Gruyere
The Brie
And the white cheese for darioles[4]

❧ 6. AUSTRIAN SALADS ☙

Austria 1719. (Hagger part 4, vol. 2, 160–167)

Hop Salad

Young hop shoots which have just appeared above ground, or similar tips, cleaned and blanched like asparagus, make a good salad.

Elder Shoot Salad

Green elder shoots, plucked in the spring, blanched and dressed with pepper, vinegar and oil, are good, but too much will cause purging.

Stinging Nettle Salad

The tips of the larger variety of stinging nettle, cleaned, blanched like asparagus and strained, then dressed when cold with vinegar and oil, make a good salad.

Tongue and Ham Salad

Tongue and all kinds of smoked sausage, thinly sliced, are good with vinegar and oil.

The simple salad recipes above are from the magisterial Austrian cookbook *Neues saltzburgisches koch-buch* (Augsburg, 1719), written by Conrad Hagger, master cook to the Archbishop of Salzburg. The meat-rich tongue and ham salad is very typical of Austrian cuisine.

➥ 7. ROYAL SALAD FROM LABRADA ⬱

Spain 1747. (de La Mata, 162)

Mince endive and lettuce, mixed with peeled apples, a few good herbs, onions and celery, also chopped, arrange in a dish, forming in every quarter, arches and other figures, according to the structure of your design: proceed to garnish the salad with pomegranate kernels, pine nuts, fine capers, chopped egg white and yolks, parsley and onion in quarters, some slices of green lemons with their rinds sculpted, anise comfits, citron cut in little sticks, cleaned anchovies, olives made rabbits, and curly celery placed in the middle. Having arranged all these according to taste, season a little before serving with the bones that have been reserved from anchovies, three cloves of garlic, a bit of cumin and oregano, dissolved in a pot with a little vinegar, to which is added olive oil, sugar, a little more vinegar if necessary, and pepper: sprinkle this on the plate a little before it is carried to the table.

To garnish this Salad, you can make use of buds from Lettuce, distributed around the edge of the Salad.

This dish may have originated in a district in Galicia in northwest Spain called Labrada. What is not mentioned in the recipe is the practice of building up the ingredients on a foundation of Gazpacho (recipe 21). Like an English Grand Salad, it was arranged with elegance, the various salad stuffs being laid out on the plate in the form of arches and geometrical shapes. What is probably meant here are whole carved lemons (rather than the jagged lemons of recipe 3). Elaborately carved fruits were very popular in high-status cooking during the seventeenth century and were used to garnish many kinds of dishes.

SOUPS

➥ 8. THE QUEEN'S POTTAGE ⬱

France 1651. (La Varenne, 9)

Take almonds, beat them and stew them in a good stock, a bouquet of herbs, the flesh of a lemon and a small quantity of breadcrumbs. Season them with salt, taking care they do not burn, stir them very often and strain them. Then take your bread and gently cook it in the best broth, which you will make as follows. After you have taken the bones out of some roasted partridge or capon, beat them in a mortar. Then take some good stock and simmer the bones with mushrooms and strain them through a cloth. Simmer your bread in this stock and as it simmers, sprinkle it with both the almond stock and meat stock. Then put into it some minced partridge or capon flesh, until it is full. Then take a red-hot fire shovel and pass it over it. Garnish your pottage with cockscombs, pistachios, pomegranate kernels and meat stock, and serve.

This soup is an imaginative variation on a basic chicken or partridge broth. It has some lingering medieval elements, such as the almond-milk stock. However, a simple bouquet of herbs is used instead of the pungent spice mixture that would have flavored a pottage of this kind in medieval times. Simmering bread in broths and pottages had been an important part of the soup-making process for centuries and was occasionally carried out at the table in a chafing dish. The inclusion of mushrooms to heighten the flavor is very typical of the new emerging style of high-status French cookery, as is the colorful garnish of pistachios, cockscombs, and pomegranate seeds. These were used to embellish the wide rim of the large plate from which pottages were served in this period, as the soup tureen had not yet been invented.

Toasting the surface of the soup with a red-hot fire shovel produces a brown and delicious skin, on which could also be floated a few pistachio nuts and pomegranate seeds. Browning the soup was also carried out with a specialized tool called a salamander. This recipe was disseminated throughout Europe in translations of La Varenne.

❧ 9. CAPON POTTAGE WITH BRIGNOLLE PRUNES ☙

France 1656. (de Lune, 183)

Cook some prunes in a little pot with some good bouillon, Levantine dates, season with salt, a few cloves. Pass some of the prunes through a sieve. Make the potage by cooking it carefully with bread crusts, garnish with prunes and pour in the strained prunes and some gravy.

Combinations of fruit and meat were common in medieval and Renaissance cooking. They lingered into the seventeenth century, but had little appeal to the discerning palates of eighteenth-century French diners and they start to vanish from the cookbooks by the 1730s. This very simple chicken pottage is thickened with a purée of Brignolle prunes. These celebrated prunes are still grown today around the town of Brignolle in Provence. The famous Cock-a-Leekie soup of Scotland originally contained prunes and is a close relative of this dish.

⇥ 10. MINESTRA OF PARTRIDGES ⇤

Italy (Mantua) 1662. (Stefani, 27)

Take three partridges, and put them on a spit, baste them frequently with butter, and when they are cooked, draw out the spit, and remove the meat, mince it finely with grated bread, and then take the bones from the partridges, and pound them in the mortar, take this juice, which you have expressed, add six ounces of pine nuts, four ounces of melon seeds, and dissolve all in rich broth, and when it is well dissolved, pass it through a sieve, and with this sauce put the partridge to the fire, but take care that the broth covers the minced partridge by the depth of two fingers, and then you add three ounces of candied citron, two ounces of fine sugar, six ounces of thick cream, four egg yolks, cook on a gentle fire, and always stir with a wooden spoon, and to finish you add a little nutmeg, the juice of three lemons, which makes a delicious and very exquisite soup, serve hot, with slices of Spanish bread below, and above sugar and cinnamon.

A *minestra* was a thick, hearty Italian soup. It is said to have gotten its name because it was formerly served at table by the head of the household, who literally "ministered" the soup. The next three *minestre* recipes are from *l'Arte di ben cucinare* (1662) by Bartolomeo Stefani, a Bolognese cook who worked at the court of the Gonzaga family in Mantua. The pinnacle of Stefani's career was a banquet he cooked for Queen Christina of Sweden in November 1655.

This *minestra* is made from the minced flesh of the *starna*, or English partridge (*Pedrix pedrix*), a popular game bird in Italy at this period. A highly flavored juice was expressed from the bones of the partridges using a special utensil called a duck press or *susidio*. The *minestra*, which is thickened with pine nuts and decorticated melon seeds, is seasoned (rather than sweetened) with a small quantity of sugar. This sugar seasoning was used to bring out the flavors of the other ingredients and to allay the acidity of the lemon juice. Spanish bread (*pane di Spagna*) was a kind of biscuit rather like a sponge finger that sat at the bottom of the soup bowl (see recipe 148).

⇥ 11. MINESTRA OF PUMPKIN ⇤

Italy (Mantua) 1662. (Stefani, 27)

Take a pumpkin simmered in broth and pass it through a sieve; take six ounces of almonds pounded in a mortar with a glass of milk; pass this also through a sieve and put with the pumpkin to cook in fat chicken stock: and when the pumpkin soup is ready, put in four egg yolks and the juice of four oranges to make it tasty.

The orange juice in this simple pumpkin soup would have been squeezed from bitter oranges of the type we now call Seville or marmalade oranges.

Although they have a short season in January and February, these oranges can be stored all year in a freezer.

⇥ 12. VEVER OLLIE, OR CHEESE POTTAGE ⇤

England 1661. (Rabisha, 289)

Take a pottle of strong broth, or fair water in a skillet or pipkin, set it on a clear fire to boil, put to it half a penny manchet grated, a little quantity of grated cheese, season it with pepper and a blade of mace; let them boil together half an hour, having half a pound of parmesan or well relished cheese, let it have one warm, remember some parsley, pennyroyal, and beets, small minced, put in at the first, and when you are ready to take it off, put to it the yolks of six eggs, a quarter of a pound of sweet butter beaten well together, dish them with sippets, and send it up with grated cheese about the dish.

Soups flavored with cheese were popular all over Europe at this time, and although local cheeses were used in many of them, Parmesan was the ingredient of choice for those who could afford it. The origin of the curious name for this dish is a mystery. Pennyroyal (*Mentha pulegium*) was a popular herb in English cookery, though it was more normally used to flavor forcemeats, sausages, and savory puddings, thus its popular name—pudding grass. It has a sharp minty flavor. A little mint would make a good substitute. A pottle was equivalent to two quarts, or half a gallon. Sippets were small, usually triangular pieces of toasted bread.

⇥ 13. OYSTER POTTAGE ⇤

France 1691. (Massialot, 207)

It would be requisite to fry the oysters in burnt butter, and to reserve their liquor, as it has elsewhere been observed: at the same time, you must also fry with your oysters, some mushrooms cut into pieces, and a little flour, and afterwards let all boil in strained pea soup, with salt and a piece of green lemon: then the bread being soaked in good fish-bouillon, and the oysters and mushrooms cooked, they may be garnished with capers and lemon slices, and so served up, after having poured the oyster-liquor into the potage, with the juices of mushrooms and lemons.

This, and the following recipe, is a meager soup designed for fish days. Make the pea soup by frying some finely chopped onion in a little butter until they are cooked, but not brown. Add three or more cups of fresh garden or frozen peas and cover with some good vegetable stock. Simmer until the peas are tender, and then turn the whole mixture into a purée. Make your fish stock for soaking the bread by cooking some fish bones, heads, and other cheap pieces of fish in water with a bundle of herbs—strain and season to taste. Once you have made these two preparations, it is easy to follow Massialot's instructions.

ᴈ 14. PURSLANE POTTAGE ꝫ

France 1691. (Massialot, 164)

The purslane, if it be small, must be laid whole length into a little pot, and boiled in broth, or pea soup, with an onion stuck with cloves, a carrot, a few parsnips, and a thickening liquor: when it is ready, and the crusts are well soaked, the potage may be garnished in the usual manner.

Purslane (*Portulaca oleracea* L.) is a succulent salad herb that was popular throughout Europe. It has delicious fleshy stems and was used a great deal in French dishes designed to be eaten on days when meat was forbidden by the church.

ᴈ 15. ZUPPA ALLA REALE ꝫ

Italy (Kingdom of Naples) 1692. (Latini, vol. 1, 304)

You make a zuppa, with white bread, with breast of capon, hot spicy salami, layered with slices of prosciutto, fried golden in butter, soaked in good capon broth, covered with slices of Provatura or mozzarella cheese, toasted, and then put on top of the said bread with cream; you serve it hot with good parmesan cheese on top.

This is a typical *zuppa* from Baroque Naples. It is hardly what we would today call a soup, being more like a lasagna that has been made with fried bread instead of pasta. The topping of cheese would have been toasted with a fire shovel or salamander. Various sweet sponge biscuits like *pane di Spagna* were often used in *zuppe* instead of bread. Capon breast, turkey, and veal were the favored meats, but pigeon and other game birds were occasionally also used. A *zuppa* could also be a sweet dish. Bartolomeo Stefani describes one made by layering *cantucci* biscuits soaked in Malvasia wine below a purée of peaches garnished with jasmine flowers and chopped pistachios.[5] Sweet *zuppe* like these were the precursors of modern layered trifle dishes like *zuppa inglese* and tiramisu.

ᴈ 16. MINESTRA OF AUBERGINES ꝫ

Italy (Kingdom of Naples) 1694. (Latini, vol. 2, 55)

Cut the aubergines in little pieces, with onion minced small, and zucchini, and little pieces of tomato; fry everything together, with your sweet herbs, with unripe grapes when in season and with the usual spices, this will turn out a very good dish in the Spanish manner.

Antonio Latini, the author of this recipe, was a *scalco* or house steward who ran the household affairs of Don Stefano Carillo y Salcedo, the Spanish regent of Naples. He included a few recipes that required tomatoes in his remarkable book *Lo scalco alla moderna* of 1692, the first Italian cookbook to do so. All of these are dishes "in the Spanish manner," testifying to the fact that the Spanish introduced the tomato into the Neapolitan culinary tradition. For centuries, unripe grapes had commonly been included in innumerable Italian dishes to provide a tart flavor without citrus overtones. They were eventually superseded in Naples by the tomato. In this fledgling ratatouille we see both the old and new being used in the same dish. By the "usual spices" Stefani means cinnamon, cloves, and nutmeg.

᪥ 17. A SOUP WITH DUCK, WESTPHALIAN BROWN CABBAGE, SMOKED SAUSAGE, AND JUS ᪣

Austria 1719. (Hagger part 1, vol. 1, 10–11)

Pluck, clean, season and brown the ducks, cover and simmer in a lightly salted meat stock. Make a jus or brown broth from beef and good bacon. Take the brown cabbage and discard the old, tough leaves and the stem, but pull the good leaves apart one by one till you get to the tip, which you also use. Rinse and cook in fresh water like any other cabbage, strain and press out the water and season with pepper, a little garlic and nutmeg. Add a piece of bacon or an onion studded with cloves. Now take a fair amount of butter or bacon fat in a pan, cook a small quantity of flour until yellow, add the cabbage, stir a few times, then pour over it a good meat broth with plenty of fat on the surface, add the rinsed smoked sausage and bring to the boil. Press the jus through a fine sieve and add the fat from the top to the cabbage. Arrange slices of toasted bread on the serving dish, pour on a little of the jus and leave to soak in, then place the ducks in the middle, drain the liquid from the cabbage, stir and place it on the soup around the ducks. Slice the sausage thinly and decorate the dish with it, and the soup is ready to serve.

With its smoked sausage and cabbage, this hearty duck soup is very typical of Austrian and German cooking. Westphalian brown cabbage is curly kale. A lean wild duck like a mallard or widgeon, or a pair of teal, would be ideal for this recipe. Use *katenrauchwurst* or other coarse smoked sausage. See recipe 177 for directions to make jus.

᪥ 18. A GREEN SOUP WITH STUFFED CHICKENS ᪣

Austria 1719. (Hagger part 1, vol. 1, 46–47)

First take well-cleaned chickens, as many as you need for the soup. Press in the ribs or breast with the thumb and insert a finger underneath, pulling the skin off bit by bit. Now add the following stuffing: pick clean and finely chop a large quantity of parsley, fry it briefly in butter, add an egg and stir, pour out on to a board and add fresh bone marrow, bread softened in cream, mace and salt, and also more eggs, being careful that the mix is neither too firm nor too soft. Put the mix in a syringe and use it to stuff the chickens. Cut the feet off at the knees and insert the syringe at the tail end, tuck the head under one wing and place the chicken on its back in a suitable dish, pour on meat broth, add an onion studded with cloves and cook on a moderate heat. Take freshly-shelled peas and after they have been cleaned and washed, place them in a pan with a good-sized lump of butter, finely chopped parsley and pepper, add meat broth, cover and boil quickly but not too long, or they will spoil. Cut some pieces of bread and brown them with finely chopped parsley in butter or bacon fat. These will be stirred into the peas before serving and should reach the table still quite crisp. Make some little finger-length rolls of dumpling paste with some chicory, all cut to the same length, place in a pan greased with butter, add a little cream or meat broth, heat from above and beneath or place in a warm oven, then sprinkle them with pistachios. Arrange the items as follows: first the peas with the pieces of bread, the chickens in the middle, the tail end inwards, the little dumplings around the outside like stars, and the whole decorated with Genoese pasties.

At this period it was common kitchen practice to stuff chickens with forcemeat by inserting it under the skin which covers their breasts. As described here, this was done with a large syringe, a kitchen utensil that was also used to squirt batter into boiling fat to make fritters. Dumplings have been a major feature of Austrian cooking since the medieval period. To make the dough for the chicory dumplings use Hagger's recipe for spinach noodles (recipe 46), but substitute the spinach with some finely chopped chicory leaves. The dumplings here were cooked in a pan that would be equivalent to a dutch oven with hot embers below and on the lid. The soup tureen was just coming into use in this period, but was restricted to France. In most other European countries soups and pottages were served in large deep dishes with broad rims. The soup was garnished by decorating the rim of the dish. This particular dish has a complex garnish of concentric rings of dumplings and little decorated Genoese pies or petit patties. It seems strange today, but soups were often dressed with little pies like these. In England, small pies called chewitts were used to adorn elaborate bisques and terrines. See recipe 62 for Hagger's instructions to make Genoese pastries.

⊰ 19. PLUM POTTAGE ⊱

England c. 1720. (Kidder, F4)

Take 2 gallons of strong broth; put to it to a pound of currents, two pound of raisins of the Sun, half an ounce of sweet spice, a pound of sugar, a quart of claret, a pint of sack (a Spanish white wine), the juice of three oranges and three lemons; thicken it with grated bisket, or rice flour with a pound of prunes.

This rich and fruity broth was once the chief dish of the English Christmas table. It was also called Christmas Porridge but is now extinct in Britain. Its gradual decline during the course of the eighteenth century maps the radical shift in taste that occurred during the period covered by this book. In the 1650s spicy meat dishes cooked with fruit and seasoned with sugar were still popular in most European countries, including France. A century later they had almost disappeared, though some, like this soup, survived for a time as a marooned vestige of medieval cuisine. In 1760, the cookbook author Martha Bradley wrote,

> This is a famous old English Dish, and though at present disused in London, yet as there are many Families in the Country who still keep up the Custom of Hospitality, and admit this among the Entertainments of the Season....The French laugh outrageously at this old English Dish, and to be sure it is an odd Medley.[6]

At the time of La Varenne and Pierre de Lune the French were happy to dine on sweet-sour meat based dishes like capon soup with Brignolle prunes, but by the middle of the eighteenth century most Frenchmen would have been horrified by dishes of this kind. By this time, the differentiation between sweet and savory was complete.

◁ 20. POTTAGE OF RED HERRINGS ▷

England 1730. (Carter, 29)

First make a stock of meager soup, with herbs, and roots, and bread, and season it with the same seasoning, but not too much salt: take six red herrings, and broil them and beat them in a mortar; put to them some of your stock, and strain and force them through your strainer; make a ragoût of old onions, and strain them into the rest; take a little celery and endive, a little spinach, sorrel, and parsley; mince them, and pass them in brown butter thickened until very tender; puts altogether, and stove it up; put in fried French manchet, dish it up, and broil some more red herrings, and lay them round the dish; and garnish with sliced lemon, and scalded spinach.

Red herrings were salted and smoked herrings that were made on the east coast of England. They were often given away free in alehouses because their saltiness tended to induce thirst and encouraged customers to buy a great deal of beer. This is why Charles Carter states not to put too much salt in the stock. True red herrings are no longer made. The closest substitutes are bloaters or kippers. If you can get hold of these they make a very good, smoky fish soup. The herrings were broiled or grilled over the coals on an implement called a gridiron and then stripped of their bones before being pushed through a sieve. A ragoût of old onions is simply an onion purée. The word *pass* means to gently fry or sauté. The soup is finished with croutons of fried white bread (French manchet) and the rim of the dish is garnished with more herrings, lemon slices, and cooked spinach.

◆ 21. GAZPACHOS OF ALL KINDS ◆

Spain 1747. (de La Mata, 164)

The most common gazpacho is called Capon de Galera, which is made thus: grate a pound of crust of a loaf of bread, toasted and without the soft crumb, soak in water: then toss it in a salsa, consisting of anchovies, and a couple of cloves of garlic, grinding them together, with vinegar, sugar, salt and olive oil; when everything is well mixed, leave to soften the bread with the garlic: after it has been put on the plate, incorporate all or part of the range and vegetables from the Royal Salad.

Another less expensive mode is to pound the garlic with just a bit of lemon chopped, olive oil, and sugar, garnish the gazpacho the same as before.

As well as being served on its own as a soup, gazpacho was incorporated into salads, such as the Royal Salad from Labrada (see recipe 7). Modern gazpacho usually contains bell peppers, tomatoes, and cucumbers. These additions are almost certainly derived from the practice of garnishing the simple bread and garlic gazpacho with various salad vegetables. It is traditional to use week-old bread for making gazpacho. Pound the ingredients together with a mortar and pestle.

MEAT

◆ 22. FOIE GRAS BAKED IN EMBERS ◆

France 1651. (La Varenne, 61)

Bard foie gras with bacon fat, and season it well with salt, pepper, ground cloves, and a small bouquet of herbs. Then wrap it in four or five sheets of paper, and put it to roast in the embers like a quince. When it is baked, be careful not to lose the sauce. Take the outermost sheets of paper and serve it on the inside paper, or if you prefer on a plate.

It was common practice to wrap quinces in two or three layers of wet paper and roast them in the hot embers of a wood fire (see recipe 77). Some vegetables like Jerusalem artichokes and skirrets were also cooked in this way. If you do not want to use foie gras, chicken or lamb's liver can be cooked using this method. The outer paper will get charred, but the sheets within are protected from the heat.

⋺ 23. LAMB RAGOÛT ⋲

France 1656. (de Lune, 38)

Cut it [the lamb] into four quarters, lard it with medium sized lardoons, and give a little color to it, put it in a terrine with seasoned bouillon of salt, pepper, a packet, cloves, mushrooms and when it is cooked, sauté some oysters in a frying pan, a little flour, two anchovies, lemon juice and garnish with sliced fried mushrooms.

A ragoût was a strongly flavored stew that became one of the signature dishes of the new style of French cooking. Some ragoûts were complicated preparations containing expensive ingredients like truffles and morels. This one is not difficult to prepare. It is based on a boned leg of lamb cut into four quarters. Lardoons are strips of bacon fat that were sewn into the lean meat with a larding pin. Larding pins are still available from good cooking-equipment suppliers and have not changed a great deal since the days of Pierre de Lune.

⋺ 24. TO ROAST A FILLET OF BEEF ⋲

England 1660. (May, 113)

Take a fillet which is the tenderest part of the beef, and lieth in the inner part of the sirloin, cut it as big as you can, broach it on a broach not too big, and be careful not to broach it through the best of the meat, roast it leisurely, and baste it with sweet butter, set a dish to save the gravy while it roasts, then prepare sauce for it of good store of parsley, with a few sweet herbs chopped small, the yolks of three or four eggs, sometimes gross pepper minced amongst them with the peel of an orange, and a little onion; boil these together, and put in a little butter, vinegar, gravy, a spoonful of strong broth, and put it to the beef.
    Otherways.
Sprinkle it with rose-vinegar, claret-wine, elder-vinegar, beaten cloves, nutmeg, pepper, cinamon, ginger, coriander-feed, fennil-seed, and salt; beat these things fine, and season the fillet with it then roast it, and baste it with butter, save the gravy, and blow off the fat, serve it with juyce of orange or lemon, and a little elder-vinegar.

Fillet has been revered for centuries as the choicest cut of beef. These two English recipes illustrate how it was often served with a slightly acid sauce made with bitter orange or floral vinegars, such as elder or rose. These flavorings were used by cooks throughout Europe at this period in many fish and meat dishes. Broach is another name for spit, from the French word *broche*. A small, slender spit was used in order not to tear or spoil the fragile joint.

✦ A BILL OF FARE FOR CHRISTMAS DAY [IN ENGLAND], AND HOW TO SET THE MEAT IN ORDER

FIRST COURSE

Oysters

 1. A collar of brawn
 2. Stewed broth of mutton marrowbones
 3. A grand sallet
 4. A potage of caponets
 5. A breast of veal in stoffado
 6. A boiled partridge
 7. A chine of beef, or sirloin roast
 8. Minced pies
 9. A Jegote of mutton with anchovy sauce
10. A made dish of sweetbread
11. A swan roast
12. A pasty of venison
13. A kid with a pudding in his belly
14. A steak pie
15. A haunch of venison roasted
16. A turkey roast and stuck with cloves
17. A made dish of chickens in puff paste
18. Two bran geese roasted, one larded
19. Two large capons, one larded
20. A custard

THE SECOND COURSE FOR THE SAME MESS

Oranges and lemons

 1. A young lamb or kid
 2. Two couple of rabbits
 3. A pig souc't with tongues
 4. Three ducks, one larded
 5. Three pheasants, 1 larded
 6. A swan pye
 7. Three brace of partridge, three larded
 8. Made dish in puff paste
 9. Bolonia sausages, and anchovies, caviete, and pickled oysters in a dish
10. Six teels, three larded
11. A gammon of Westphalia bacon
12. Ten plovers, five larded
13. A quince pye, or warden pie
14. Six woodcocks, 3 larded
15. A standing tart in puff-paste, preserved fruits, pippins &c.

16. A dish of Larks
17. Six dried neats tongues
18. Sturgeon
19. Powdered Geese
20. Jellies[7]

⇥ 25. HOW TO MAKE A HOT POT OF EVERYTHING ⇤

Netherlands 1669. (De verstandige kock, *14)*

Take a capon, the meat of mutton, ox and pork, a small duck and some sausages. Put everything together on a fire, add some salt, skim off and stew until tender. Then add ginger and pepper, and some previously cooked Savoy cabbage. Stew together until ready.

This Dutch *hutspot* of mixed meats is the origin of the English word hotch-potch (hodgepodge), a mixture of many ingredients. It is closely related to the *olla podrida* of Spain and the *bollito misto* of Italy. Ginger was a very popular spice in Dutch cookery at this time. The author failed to explain that the ingredients needed to be covered with stock or water, but his readers would have understood that this was a standard procedure.

⇥ 26. NEAPOLITAN FILLET OF BEEF ⇤

Italy (Kingdom of Naples) 1692. (Latini, vol. 1, 135)

Here in Naples it is normal for us to cater for our guests with the best quality fillet of beef, which is really exquisite when it is dressed with oregano, cloves of crushed garlic, finely minced chilli and sufficient salt; poach with a little scented vinegar, after leaving it in this dressing for the space of five or six hours, or overnight. It will also roast well on a spit; afterwards it is cut into thin slices and served to table as it is, and it is very tasty.

This method of cooking a fillet of beef also uses floral-scented vinegar. However, with its aromatic seasoning of oregano and garlic, this is a much more Mediterranean approach to dealing with this premium cut than May's very English recipes. It is also the earliest example of an Italian meat dish that includes fresh chili.

⇥ 27. A DISH OF SCOTCH COLLOPS ⇤

England 1699. (Birkett manuscript, 11)

Take a leg of veal and slice it very thin, then beat them to make them tender, then shred a little orange peel very small, then mix a little thyme with them, and so season, then fry them, when they are fried very well, beat some yolks of eggs, and a little wine; and put them into the frying pan, and toss all together, and so dish them, and lay some shred lemon upon the top, and garnish them with what you think fit.

This is not a Scottish dish. The word scotch meant "to cut or score," referring to the practice of hacking the slices of meat with the back of a knife to make them thin and tender. This is what the author of the recipe means when she instructs readers to "beat them." A collop was a thin slice of meat and has the same meaning as escalope. The rich sauce made by cooking the collops in wine thickened with egg yolks was sometimes called a lear or caudle in the English cookbooks of this period. This was a popular dish because it was quick and easy to prepare.

⅓ 28. A SHOULDER OF MUTTON STUFFED WITH OYSTERS ⅔

England 1730. (Carter, 51)

First take your oysters, and set them, and beard them; then take some parsley, thyme, pepper, salt, and some crumbed bread; mix all these well together; then take the yolks of 4 eggs; mix up your oysters in all this; then raise a few holes, and stuff your mutton with three oysters in a hole; then cover with a mutton caul, and so roast it gently: garnish with mutton cutlets.

Combination dishes of mutton and oysters were highly esteemed in England, and this dish frequently occurs in cookbooks of the period. Minced mutton, oysters, and anchovies were also mixed together to make sausages. Mutton was ubiquitous in England but rarely eaten in France and Italy, where its strong flavor was not appreciated. To stop the oysters from falling out of their holes, the whole shoulder was wrapped in a membrane of caul fat.

⅓ 29. A SPANISH OLIO ⅔

France 1736. (La Chapelle, vols. 1, 3)

Take slices of beef from the lower part of the brisket, cut them in pieces, the bigness of two fingers, and put them in water; take also some slices of the breast of mutton, and some slices of the breast of veal, and sheep's-rumps, and cut them into handsome pieces; then garnish the stew-pot all round with slices of beef an inch thick, and put in your pieces of beef, with a good quantity of roots, a bunch of celery, very neat, because it must be used in serving up, and a bunch of leeks. Moisten the whole with broth; when the beef is well cooked, put in your slices of veal, and mutton, and sheep's-rumps, two hogs-feet and ears, two partridges, two pigeons, the knuckle of a ham, a good sausage, and half a well blanched white cabbage, drained, and tied up with packthread; season the whole with onions, put in a mignonette, and cover it with slices of beef; take two pounds of veal, cut them in slices, and set them to sweat gently over the stove, till they stick to the stew-pan, but do not let them burn; put some good broth into it, and put it in your olio. You must put to steep overnight, some garbanzo, in lukewarm water; in the morning, pick them clean, one after another, wash them in hot water, boil them in a saucepan with good broth. Your olio being done, give it the best taste, you can; and take out all your meat and roots, and put them in a large dish; range handsomely, in the dish, or olio pot, you serve up in, your cuts of beef, veal, and mutton, and roots, which must be well cleaned; when everything is in order in your dish, put in your hogs-feet and ears, cabbage celery, and leeks; add, lastly, your garbanzos, with a little olio bouillon, and serve it hot. You serve it in covered china cups, with slices of toasted bread as big as your two fingers; fill each cup with broth, and put a toast at the side. Take care your broth is well flavored; and serve it, as hot as you can.

Mignonette is made like this: take a piece of muslin, and tie up, with a little handful of coriander seeds, and pepper, a dozen of cloves, and the nutmeg; bind the mignonette and put them in your olio.

A silver tureen or olio for serving olla podrida.

This elaborate and ambitious mixed meat stew was the iconic dish of the Baroque age. It had been a symbol of princely and lavish hospitality all over Europe since the Renaissance but reached the height of its popularity in the second half of the seventeenth century. At this time it was often presented in the form of a large pyramid of meat in the center of the table, though the soup or broth was usually served as a separate dish. This particular recipe is unusual in that it explains how little covered china cups were used for this purpose. The olio or olla podrida originated in Spain and was named after the pot, or olla, in which it was cooked. It was transformed in France in the 1730s into a more streamlined dish called an *ouille*. This less-extravagant version became one of the important centerpieces of the first course and was served in a spectacular silver tureen called a *pot d'ouille*. Nowadays, it would be an impractical and expensive dish to make and is included here because it was such a revered dish during this period. The modern Spanish garbanzo stew called *puchero* is a close relative of the olio.

⊰ 30. BEEF IN A LEMON SAUCE ⊱

Germany (Nuremburg) 1691. (Nürnbergisches koch-buch, 453)

Toast one or two pieces of rye bread, simmer in meat broth and push through a sieve. Cut one or two lemons (according to the quantity of meat) into small cubes and add to the broth, add some vinegar, pepper, ginger and nutmeg, continue to simmer with a knob of butter. Pour over the cooked beef. It is also possible to pour the broth over the beef in a pot with feet, and allow it to simmer for a while, cooking the two together.

This homely recipe is typical of Nuremburg cooking at this period. The rye bread used to thicken the sauce was dark black bread that gave a slightly sour and nutty flavor to the sauce. Use black rye bread or pumpernickel. Chop the lemon into small pieces. Only a small amount of vinegar is required to accentuate the acidity of the sauce.

ᙏ 31. TO DRESS VENISON IN COLLOPS ᙓ

England 1723. (Nott, V36)

Cut part of a haunch of venison into collops, then hack it with the back of the knife, lard it with small lardoons; then mince thyme, rosemary, parsley, spinach, and other sweet herbs small with beef suet; season them with salt, cloves and nutmeg beaten, and mingle them well, together with the yolks of half a dozen eggs; spread these upon your collops, tie them together, spit them and roast them; set a dish under them to receive the gravy, put to it some claret; when the collops are roasted enough, set the dish over a chafing-dish of coals, put in grated bread, vinegar, sugar, and beaten cinnamon; stir them together, add a ladleful of drawn butter, dish your venison, and pour the sauce over them.

Collops are thin slices of meat. Venison is a very lean meat that can easily dry up when cooked on a spit in front of a hot fire. This is an unusual and effective way of cooking this difficult meat, as the lard and suet sandwiched between the venison slices ensure a succulent result. Although this recipe is from a period when the French culinary revolution was fast taking hold in Britain at court level, this dish requires a sweet-sour cinnamon sauce that had been served with venison since the days of Geoffrey Chaucer. Made with wine, vinegar, sugar, and spice, this archaic sauce was known as galantine. During the course of the eighteenth century, it would be superseded by more sophisticated creations from the imaginative new repertoire of sauces emerging in France. Like most sauces of early provenance, galantine was thickened with breadcrumbs rather than flour and was enriched with the juices from the roast.

POULTRY

ᙏ 32. CAPON WITH OYSTERS ᙓ

France 1651. (La Varenne, 76)

After your capon is dressed and barded with bacon fat, roast it with a cover of buttered paper, and as it roasts, put under it a dripping pan. After you have cleaned your oysters very well, if they are old you shall blanch them. When

*they are well cleaned and blanched, sauté them in the pan with the gravy
that has fallen from your capon, and season them with mushrooms, an onion
stuck with cloves, and a bundle of herbs. After they are well fried, you should
take out the bundle of herbs, and the rest you shall put into the body of the
capon, which you stew with a few capers, and serve.*

A capon is a castrated cockerel that has been fattened for the table. It was
considered to be the most flavorsome of all fowl. Its breast meat was also very
white and this lent it many decorative possibilities in the early modern period
kitchen. Birds were barded for the spit by covering their breasts with a *bard* or
sheet of bacon fat. This was secured by tying it on with tape or string.

⇥ 33. A WHITE FRICASSÉE OF RABBITS OR CHICKENS ⇤

England 1720. (Kidder, G1)

*Cut them in pieces and wash them from the blood and fry them on a soft fire
then put them in a tossing pan with a little strong broth: season them and
toss them up with mushrooms and oysters; when almost enough put to them
a pint of cream and thicken it with a bit of butter rolled up in flour.*

Savory Balls

*Take part of a leg of lamb or veal and scrape it fine with the same quantity
of minced beef suet, a little lean bacon, sweet herbs, a shallot and anchovy,
beat it in a mortar till it is as smooth as wax, season it with savory spice and
make it into little balls.*

These two recipes are from one of the most elegantly produced of all
English cookbooks, compiled by the "pastry master" Edward Kidder, who
ran a number of cookery schools in London in the early eighteenth century.
The recipes were printed from engraved copper plates rather than from mov-
able type and the book is illustrated with detailed engravings of pie designs.
A fricassée was a quickly made dish, where the meat was first fried and then
sautéed in a cream sauce. Although the fricassée originated in France, it had
been popular in England since the middle of the sixteenth century. The sauce
is thickened with a little ball of butter rolled in flour. A fricassée was often
served with a garnish of little meatballs. Kidder's recipe for these is included.
He states that savory spice was a mixture of salt, pepper, mace, and nutmeg.

⇥ 34. PULLETS WITH VERJUICE GRAPES ⇤

France 1746. (Menon, 123)

*Pluck, singe, and clean the pullets, stuff them inside with their livers mixed
with butter, parsley, minced chives, salt, coarsely ground pepper, and cook
them on a spit. In a casserole put a little butter, with two onions, a clove of*

garlic, parsley, chives, a carrot, a parsnip, two cloves, sauté them altogether until they are all lightly browned; add to it a good pinch of flour, wet this with a glass of bouillon, let it cook and reduce a little, rub through a sieve, take a good handful of very green verjuice grapes with the pips removed and blanched for a few moments in boiling water, remove them in order to let them drain; put them in the sauce with two egg yolks, leave on the stove to thicken without boiling, stirring them all the time, as soon as the sauce has thickened, take it off the fire. Pour over the pullets.

Verjus de grains were whole unripe grapes. They were much used in early modern European cookery to provide acidity in both savory and sweet dishes. In France the favored source of verjuice was the Bordelais grape, a variety that rarely matured and was not used much in making wine.[8] This recipe is typical of the simplified cuisine that emerged in France from the 1730s onwards. It is a very trimmed-down approach to cooking when compared with the complex court style that preceded it. Menon, who was one of the most prolific cookbook authors of the middle of the eighteenth century, targeted *La cuisinière bourgeoise* at the thrifty middle-class housewives of France. Its clear, easy-to-follow instructions made it one of the best-selling cookbooks in the second half of the eighteenth century. A hundred years before, a dish of this kind would have been seasoned with sugar to produce a sweet-sour effect. By the middle of the eighteenth century, sweet sauces for meat had become more or less obsolete. The pullets here are dressed in a savory though rather tart sauce.

FISH AND SEAFOOD

❧ 35. TO FARCE A CRAB ❧

England 1660. (May, 411)

Take a boil'd crab, take the meat out of the shell, and mince the claws with a good fresh eel, season it with cloves, mace, some sweet herbs chopped, and salt, mingle all together with some yolks of eggs, some grapes, gooseberries, or barberries, and sometimes boil'd artichocks in dice-work, or boil'd asparagus, some almond-paste, the meat of the body of the crab, and some grated bread, fill the shells with this compound, & make some into balls, bake them in a dish with some butter and white wine in a soft oven; being baked, serve them in a clean dish with a sauce made of beaten butter, large mace, scalded grapes, gooseberries, or barberries, or some slic'd orange or lemon and some yolks of raw eggs dissolved with some white-wine or claret, and beat up thick with butter; brew it well together, pour it on the fish and lay on some slic't lemon, stick the balls with some pistaches, slic't almonds, pine-apple-seed, or some pretty cuts in paste.

This imaginative and unusual way of dressing crabmeat is typical of upper-class English food of the seventeenth century. Its combination of tart fruit such as gooseberries and barberries with fish and ground almonds is harmonious and visually pleasing. The yellow of the egg yolk and the bright crimson of the barberries are very striking. Eel, an oily fish, was added for extra succulence. The little baked crabmeat balls that are spiked with pistachios, almonds, and pine nuts make a particularly attractive garnish. This dish is typical of an international court style of cookery and would equally be at home on a table in a Neapolitan palace as in an English country house.

⇥ 36. TUNA FISH STEW ⇤

Spain 1662. (Montiño, 288)

After salting, this tuna is very good for making a stew which tastes like a meat olla podrida. Simmer the tuna, then fry it for a little in big chunks. Take a stock of chick peas, add well-prepared cabbage hearts, all kind of green vegetables, and season with all kinds of spices, and caraway, then fry a little flour, but not so that it browns, and stir it in, and serve on a white soup, and serve rocket sauce with it.

With its combination of garbanzos (chickpeas) and lightly salted tuna, this is a typical dish of coastal Spain. It is a fish *olla podrida* designed for days when flesh was not allowed. Tuna was chosen for its meatlike qualities. The night before you make the *olla podrida,* cover some thick tuna steaks in coarse sea salt. The next day wash the salt off and soak the fish in slowly running water for about 30 minutes. The salting makes the flesh of the fish much firmer and more like meat. Do not use any salt in the stock in which you cook the garbanzos. Other than the caraway, which is an unusual but excellent flavoring for garbanzos, it is unclear which other spices were intended, but other fish recipes in this influential and encyclopedic book use pepper, nutmeg, and mace. Martinez Montiño's *Arte de cocina* was first published in Madrid in 1611 but it remained in print until the middle of the eighteenth century, and many of its rather archaic recipes were modified to suit prevailing taste.

⇥ 37. HOW TO FRY MUSSELS IN A PAN ⇤

Netherlands 1669. (De verstandige kock, 17)

Take mussels. Take them out of their shells alive and drain well, so that hardly any liquid is left. Then roll them in wheat flour with salt, fry in butter or oil and eat with some verjuice. This is good for the stomach.

The Dutch have always been great consumers of shellfish. This unpretentious dish is typical of the homely food of the Netherlands in the age of Rembrandt and Hals. In Holland and Britain, where grapes were not commonly grown, verjuice was often made from lightly fermented crab apple juice. This produces a less acidic condiment than vinegar, which was ideal for giving relish to fish dishes.

⊰ 38. FRIED SWORDFISH ⊱

Italy (Kingdom of Naples) 1694. (Latini, vol. 2, 69)

Clean and wash, that done cut him in slices, and after frying, arrange on the plate with tips of asparagus, first boiled and then fried, garnish the brim of the said plate with slices of lemon and pomegranate seeds.

The bright green of asparagus tips and the crimson of pomegranate kernels transform this basic dish into a visual and culinary treat. Swordfish were plentiful in the Bay of Naples. They were also served with sour grapes and gooseberries, or with a sauce made from almond milk and prawn stock and then garnished with *tarantello*, fish spawn, and truffles.

⊰ 39. TO ROAST A PIKE ⊱

England 1699. (Birkett manuscript)

Take your pike and rub him well over with salt, then take forth his guts and fat out of his belly. Then take a good quantity of sweet herbs. If your pike is large put in the greater quantity of all these things that are here named, a quantity of garlic, take some anchovies, and some butter, and all sorts of spice beaten together, mix these and fill his belly full, and so spike him on the spit, and with the spare of filling his belly, put it on a dish and a little wine, and baste him with it, then put all on the dish with him, and serve him up in that sauce; you may also put in a quantity of pickled herrings.

Early modern European diners enjoyed eating a vast range of freshwater fish. Pike was particularly popular. In English cookbooks of the seventeenth century there are numerous recipes for pike, but this fish has now almost completely disappeared from the British menu. A sweet-tasting young pike under two years of age was called a jack and was more expensive to buy than a larger fish. Pike always have an unpleasant coating of slime. In this late-seventeenth-century recipe from the handwritten receipt book of an English farmer's wife, readers are told the best way to deal with this is to rub the fish all over with salt. This removes the slippery, mucilaginous coating and makes the fish much easier to handle.

Roasting a pike on a spit is not a straightforward procedure because as soon as it is cooked it becomes soft and falls off. It was standard practice to tie the fish to the spit with splints of hazel wood secured with tape. In 1653, Isaac Walton explains how this is done:

Take four or five or six split sticks, or very thin laths, and a convenient quantity of tape or filleting; these laths are to be tied round about the Pike's body, from his head to his tail, and the tape tied somewhat thick, to prevent his breaking or falling off from the spit. And then take four or five or six split sticks, or very thin laths, and a convenient quantity of tape or filleting; these laths are to be tied round about the Pike's body, from his head to his tail, and the tape tied somewhat thick, to prevent his breaking or falling off from the spit.[9]

Garlic was a rather unusual flavoring in England in this period. The combination of pickled herring, herbs, and anchovies cooked in the fish's belly makes a sharp and relishing sauce for this subtly flavored fish.

❧ 40. STOCKFISH BOILED OR WITH MELTED TOPPING, MONASTERY STYLE ☙

Austria 1719. (Hagger part 4, vol. 1, 161)

Clean the stockfish and pick out any skin and bones, boil for a short time in water, remove from the heat, cover and leave to stand in a warm place. Before serving strain the fish, place it on a warm serving dish, sprinkle with breadcrumbs, finely chopped onions, parsley, spice and salt. Heat some fat or oil and melt or burn it over the top, and serve quickly.

Salt cod or stockfish was once of immense importance in the food culture of most European countries, especially those without a coastline like Austria. When fresh fish was unavailable, this easily stored preserved fish was a great alternative. However, after the Reformation, it gradually lost its popularity in the North. Obligatory fish days were taken less seriously in Protestant nations and stockfish became associated with popery. In monastic communities, salt cod was often stored in large quantities to provide the monks with fish meals on the many days they were not allowed to indulge in meat. Despite its distance from the sea, stockfish was very popular in Catholic Austria during the eighteenth century and it retained some of its associations with the ascetic life. Hagger's encyclopedic book gives 23 recipes for salt cod, including another with origins in a monastic kitchen— Stockfish in the Capucin Style. In contrast, there are only four recipes for salt cod in John Nott's *Cook's and Confectioner's Dictionary* (London, 1723) and three of these are translations of Catholic French recipes. Despite their prowess as a nation of sea fishermen, the Protestant English had lost their taste for this once essential food. In modern England it is almost impossible to buy, yet it is still of great importance in Portugal, Spain, and Italy, where it is known as *baccala*.

Stockfish needs to be soaked overnight in water to remove the bulk of the salt. In the past it was standard practice to break up the very hard sheets of salt cod into more manageable portions with an implement called a stockfish hammer before soaking it. The topping of breadcrumbs would have been toasted with a salamander or fire shovel.

⇥ 41. A PUPTON OF SALMON ⇤

England 1723. (Nott, S24)

Scale, skin, and bone your Salmon, lay the Flesh on the Dresser with the flesh of eels, minced mushrooms, chives and parsley, season with salt, pepper, nutmeg, and a little sweet basil: let all these be shredded very well together; beat three or four cloves with a dozen coriander seeds in a mortar, then put in the minced fish, and a sufficient quantity of butter, and pound altogether: then put a piece of crumb bread as big as your farce into cream or milk, and set it to simmer over a stove; and beat up the yolks of four eggs, and when it is thick enough, take it off, and set it cooling; then put into a mortar the yolks of four or five raw eggs, and the bread and cream when it is cold, pounded all well together, then make a ragoût of salmon as follows: take small mushrooms, peel them and take a slice or two of Salmon rubbed with melted butter, and broiled: then put butter into a sauce-pan, and set it over a stove till it is melted, then brown it with a little flour; put your mushrooms into it, and let them have a few turns over the stove, then put in some fish broth, salt, pepper, and a faggot of sweet herbs; take the skin off the slices of Salmon that you broil, cut it into little long slices, and put them into the sauce to the mushroom, etc. Add also some crayfish tails, and blanched asparagus tops, and let them simmer together for a while; when your ragoût is enough, take off all the fat, and set it at cooling; then rub a sauce-pan with fresh butter, butter a sheet of paper, and lay over the bottom and sides of it; spread some of the farce over it an inch thick or more; beat up an egg, and rub it over with it to make the farce lie the smoother; place the ragoût of salmon in the bottom, and cover the pupton with the same farce; rub it over with beaten egg, and bake it in an oven or baking cover, with fire over and under it; when it is baked, turn it upside down into the dish into which you intend to serve it; take off the paper, make a hole in the top, of the size of a five shilling piece, pour in some coulis of crayfish, and serve it up the table hot for a dish of the first course.

A pupton, sometimes known as a pulpatoon, was an English version of a French dish called a *poupeton*. This was a kind of pie, though the crust was made with a mixture of mincemeat and breadcrumbs called a farce, rather than pastry, and it was baked in a special mold called a *poupetonière*. This was probably dome-shaped, because the origin of the word *poupeton* is a Provençal slang word for "breast." Most recipes were meat-based and resembled a hollow meatloaf filled with game birds cooked in a ragoût or sauce. *Poupetons* of pigeons, buntings, and partridges were very popular. This pupton of salmon seems to be an invention of John Nott himself and has no French precursors. It is a complex dish, but well worth the trouble. The farce for the crust is made from a mixture of salmon and eel flesh. If you cannot obtain eel, use any other white fish—haddock or cod is suitable. The minced fish is then blended with the breadcrumbs cooked in cream or milk, a preparation known as a panada. Once this is mixed with the other ingredients to make the farce, you use it to line a mold or saucepan that has an inside layer of greased paper, reserving some of the mixture to make your cover. You fill this with the salmon, asparagus, etc. and then seal the top of the pupton with more farce.

VEGETABLES AND FUNGI

◅ 42. SALSIFY WITH BROWN BUTTER ▻

France 1656. (de Lune, 45)

Cut the salsify in rounds, toss them in a frying pan with brown butter, season with salt, pepper, nutmeg, fine herbs, a little fried flour and a splash of vinegar, and serve.

Salsify was a very popular root vegetable in seventeenth-century France. Its close relative scorzonera, or Spanish salsify, was just beginning to be grown in French gardens at this time. Nicholas de Bonnefons, a contemporary of Pierre de Lune, claims to have been one of the first Frenchmen to grow this new type of salsify, which became an immensely popular vegetable over the next century.[10] Clean and peel the salsify before you cut it across into thin rounds. Brown butter is simply butter that is heated to such a temperature that it starts to color—however, do not burn it.

◅ 43. A DISH OF EGGPLANTS ▻

Italy (Mantua) 1662. (Stefani, 84)

The eggplants are a certain fruit that are fostered in the gardens of those that have a religious vocation, like the Capuchins, the Oliervanti and others. When they are in perfection for serving, they become a dark purple in color, and polished like ivory; they are of the size of an apple and oval in shape. Take these, and remove from them the skin with exact diligence, cut open and remove the seeds, then divide into pieces, soak in fresh water, which you do two or three times to remove their natural bitterness. Remove from the water and wipe dry, put them in a pot of the correct size, with oil, salt and pepper, and put it to a charcoal fire, stirring frequently. When it is cooked, take three ounces of Ambrosian almonds for every pound of eggplant, toast on an oven peel, taking care that they don't burn, and crush them in a mortar, adding a little nutmeg and a little sugar at your discretion, and stir the whole with sour orange juice, put it in the pot with the eggplants, which you finally arrange on the plates and serve hot. It is desirable to season this dish with butter, served on top, but instead of salsa of almonds, season it with Piacentino cheese, and cinnamon on top.

Eggplants started to become a feature of southern Italian cookery in the fifteenth century. However, they do not seem to have been so well known in the North, as Stefani takes some trouble in this recipe to describe them to his Mantuan readers. Ambrosian almonds were a popular variety of sweet almonds. Toast some sweet almonds in a frying pan and crush them into a paste in a mortar with a little nutmeg, sugar, and Seville orange juice. Stefani's alternative dressing uses Piacentino cheese, which is a strong grana-type cheese made in the countryside around the city of Piacenza. If this is not available, use grana padana or a strong pecorino.

᚛ 44. TO FRY PARSNIPS ᚜

England 1699. (Birkett manuscript, 39)

Let them first be tender boiled, and if they be thick, cleave them, being peeled, strew a little beaten cinnamon on them, and put them to steep in a little sack, fry them in a little butter, make sauce with butter, sack and cinnamon beaten together and they will eat well.

This simple recipe is an excellent way of serving this sweet vegetable. Boil the parsnips first, cutting up or "cleaving" any large ones. Marinate them with a little powdered cinnamon and some dry sherry. Drain off the sherry and fry them in butter. Dress them in a sauce made with a little butter, dry sherry, and sugar beaten together in a saucepan until they form an emulsion.

᚛ 45. WARM CUCUMBER WITH PARMESAN ᚜

Austria 1719. (Hagger part 4, vol. 2, 134)

Peel the cucumbers, split them and scoop out the seeds, cook till soft in salted water or other liquid with parsley, onion and other good herbs, strain, place in a serving dish with a little meat or pea broth, sprinkle with seasoning, butter and grated parmesan cheese and serve warm.

In modern times we tend to eat cucumbers raw in salads. In the eighteenth century they were cooked in ragoûts and in many diverse ways. This is a particularly effective method of serving this delicate vegetable devised by the cook to the Archbishop of Salzburg. Gently cook the cucumbers in stock rather than water. They are particularly good when served in the pea soup option. Pea broth was a popular stock in Hapsburg cookery for fish-day dishes; a meat stock variant would have been for a flesh day. Parmesan was very popular throughout Europe during this period, but Austria's close proximity to northern Italy ensured it was a ubiquitous ingredient in the cooking of Salzburg and Vienna.

⊰ 46. SPINACH NOODLES OR DUMPLINGS ⊱

Austria 1719. (Hagger part 4, vol. 2, 26)

Blanch the spinach, chop finely, and fry in fat or butter. Take an equal quantity of grated breadcrumbs, stir together in a basin, beat in three or four eggs, add a little cream (and a spoonful of grated cheese, if liked) and seasoning. Leave to stand a while to let the mixture blend, then take white flour and a pastry board and make into noodles the thickness of a thumb. Bring salted water to the boil in a large pan, add the noodles, place on the heat but do not boil too fast, or the noodles will disintegrate. When they are cooked, lift them from the water on a spoon and place on a serving dish, sprinkle with grated cheese, breadcrumbs and melted butter.

Knödeln, or dumplings, are a traditional feature of Austro-Hungarian cuisine. They are closely related to the gnocchi and ravioli nudi of Italy. It is important to knead enough flour into the mixture before cooking the dumplings to help them hold together, but not so much that they become heavy. Roll the paste out into long sausage shapes about the thickness of your thumb and cut them into one-inch lengths. They need to be gently cooked in simmering water for just a few minutes.

⊰ 47. MORELS WITH CREAM ⊱

France 1736. (La Chapelle, vol. 3, 293)

Cut them in slices, wash them in several waters, and toss them in melted bacon, or butter, and a bunch of sweet herbs; strew over them a dust of flour, moisten them with a little bouillon, season them with salt and pepper, and let them stew; put in two spoonfuls of white coulis, if you have any, and thicken your sauce with the yolks of eggs, mixed with cream, a little nutmeg, and parsley cut small; let your ragoût be of good flavor, take a round crust of bread, rub it with good butter, and brown it before the fire; then put it into your dish, with your ragoût over it, and serve it up hot.

This is a highly flavored ragoût of morels served up on a large crouton of buttery toasted bread. The procedure is very typical of the methodical French cookery of this period, where essential ingredients like bouillon or coulis were always at hand. It is an easy dish to prepare if you have some ready-prepared coulis (see recipe 133).

⚜ 48. CARDOONS ⚜

France 1737. (l'Ecole parfaite, 400)

Take some cardoons and carefully peel them, then cut them into pieces and blanch them in water with a piece of bread. Having done that, drain your cardoons, and place them in the saucepan with beef jus, minced beef marrow, a packet of fine herbs, salt and pepper. Let it all cook together carefully, being cooked just right and well degreased, serve them up as an entremets for a meat day, with lemon juice or a trickle of verjuice.

Cardoons à Dame Claude

You prepare some cardoons as already stated, cook them in rich bouillon and beef jus, salt pepper and a bouquet of fine herbs; once cooked, serve them hot for entremets; serve them with a white sauce, with good fresh butter, salt, pepper and a drop of vinegar.

Cardoons are the blanched stems of a relative of the globe artichoke. The great French gardener Jean-Baptiste de la Quintinye cultivated them in the kitchen gardens at Versailles for Louis XIV. At this period, the cardoons were tied up with tape and then blanched by covering them with straw to exclude the light. They were usually ready for the kitchen in three weeks to a month. These two cardoon recipes look similar, but the second is dressed in a white sauce—use a béchamel (recipe 181). Beef jus is the strongly flavored gravy that naturally oozes from a roasted joint, though it was also made in other ways (see recipe 177).

⚜ 49. TO FARCE MUSHROOMS ⚜

England 1744. (Adam's Luxury, 146)

Make a farce with veal, bacon, beef marrow, French roll soaked in cream, and the yolks of two eggs, season with salt, pepper, and nutmeg. Pick the mushrooms well, and pull off the stalks, then farce them with this farce; put them in a tart-pan, and bake them in an oven: when done, dish them, and pour to them some beef gravy. You may, if you think proper, make your farce of the flesh of fish.

Veal was the choice meat for making a stuffing or farce. When well seasoned with salt, pepper, and herbs it has a subtle but flavorsome savor. The addition of beef marrow (the fat inside large bones) ensures that the mixture is succulent, as veal is a lean, rather dry meat. If you cannot get hold of beef marrow, use a little suet or butter. Large freshly harvested wild mushrooms are excellent prepared in this way.

⊰ 50. TO FRY THE ROOTS OF RED BEETS ⊱

England 1736. (Bradley, 138)

Wash your Beet-Roots, and lay them in an earthen glazed Pan, bake them in an Oven, and then peel the Skin off them: after this is done, slit them from the Top to the Tail, and cut them in the shape of the Fish call'd a Sole, about the thickness of the third part of an Inch; dip these in a thick Batter, made of White-Wine, fine Flower, sweet Cream, the Whites and Yolks of Eggs, rather more Yolks than Whites, some Pepper, Salt, and Cloves beaten fine, all well mix'd. As you dip every piece of Beet-Root in this Batter, strew them over thick with fine Flower mix'd with grated Bread, and Parsley shred small, and then fry them in Lard: when they are enough, let them dry, and serve them with a Garnish of Lemmon. They likewise may be put about stew'd Carps, Tench, or roasted Jacks, by way of Garnish, with scraped Horse-Radish, and pickled Barberries.

Richard Bradley, who was the first professor of botany at the University of Cambridge, lifted this recipe from Patrick Lamb's *Royal Cookery* (London, 1711). Lamb worked at the English Court for over 50 years, so this spectacular dish may have been a favorite of the late Stuart monarchs. Lamb, however, omits to tell us that it was an accompaniment for fish, such as roasted jack (see recipe 39). The instructions are clear, but the beetroot fritters need to be drained on some kitchen paper after they are removed from the frying pan. Although it is not a fashionable cooking vehicle today, hog's lard is the best fat in which to fry the beets. It drains off more efficiently and gives a crisper finish. The contrast of the bright green of the fried parsley and the crimson of the beetroots is striking.

⊰ 51. RECEIPTS TO DRESS POTATOES ⊱

England 1744. (Adam's Luxury, 164)

Some people when they are boil'd, have a sauce ready to put over them, made with butter, salt, and pepper; others use gravy sauces, others ketchup, and some eat them boiled with only pepper and salt; some cut the large ones in slices, and fry them with onions, others stew them with salt, pepper, ale, or water. It is a common way also to boil them first, and then peel them, and lay them in the dripping pan under roasting meat. Another way very much used in Wales, is to bake them with herrings, mixed with layers of pepper, vinegar, salt, sweet herbs, and water. Also, they cut mutton in slices, and lay them in a pan, and on them potatoes and spices, then another layer of all the same with half a pint of water; this they stew, covering all with cloths around the stew-pan, and account it excellent. The Irish have several ways of eating them: the poorer sort eat them with salt only, after they are boiled; others with butter and salt, but most with milk and sugar. Also, when they can get a piece of pork, bacon, or salt beef, they account it excellent with boiled potatoes.

Another way, *Is to mash boiled potatoes, and then put them into bacon or pork broth, with spice, pepper, and sweet herbs, which is something like pease soup.*

Another way, *Is to mash boiled potatoes very fine; then take sweet herbs dry and beaten small, with spice, butter, and salt, mixed all together. This is an excellent pudding to put in the bellies of rabbits, hares, fish etc, when roasted.*

Another way, *Is to mash them after the potatoes are boiled, and then with a mixture of other ingredients, they will make a composition for skin-puddings.*

Another way. *Potatoes boiled, pulped, and mixed with milk and salt into a dough, will make good cakes to bake.*

France and Italy were very slow to adopt potatoes as a staple food for humans. Because they thrive in the cool, wet climate of Ireland and the northwest of England, it was the Irish and British who first recognized the full potential of this vegetable. This early account of their use in British cookery is fascinating and rich with excellent ways of cooking them. Many of these dishes are still popular in the British Isles.

EGGS AND DAIRY

੩ 52. EGGS À LA INTRIGUE ੩

France 1662. (l'Escole parfaite des officiers de bouche, 345)

Put in a bowl a dozen and a half raw eggs, beat them well with two pots of cream, some salt, some pepper, some onion and some sweet herbs; put some clarified butter in a tart pan on a gentle fire; when it is hot, put in a third part of the eggs that you have beaten; when they are half cooked make a bed of pieces of cheese, of anchovies also in pieces, and some poached eggs; that done, pour on again a portion of your beaten eggs and cover the tart pan; when the eggs are almost cooked, make another bed in the same fashion; to close, put over the rest of your eggs, with little pieces of butter and grated cheese, cook well to a fine colour and serve it with lemon juice.

This unusual recipe demonstrates how it is sometimes difficult to interpret old instructions because of archaic units of volume and weight. To make what is in effect a very large type of omelet, we are told to mix two pots of cream with 18 beaten eggs. A "pot" was a unit of measurement for wine and other liquids, but it varied in size in different parts of France. The "Paris Standard" pot was equivalent to 1.86 liters, while the pot of "Toulon and Marseille" was equal to 1.07 liters. If you use a Paris pot to make this dish, the eggs remain very sloppy, because there is too much cream. However, if you use a Marseille pot it works very well. Perhaps the dish originated in the south of France. The quantities here are enormous—they could easily be divided by four. The name *à la Intrigue* may come from the fact that whole poached eggs and anchovies were hidden inside this large tortilla-like omelet. Brie cheese makes a soft and creamy filling for this dish.

53. BLANCHED MANCHET TO BE MADE IN A FRYING PAN

England 1680s. (Rainbow manuscript, 85)

Break 8 or 9 eggs, take away the whites of 4 of them, beat them with half a pint of sweet cream, put to them half a penny manchet grated, 2 ounces of sugar, nutmeg, & mace, & little rose-water: fry these with sweet butter, like a tansy: but let it be a small frying pan, that it may be thick, when tis fried wash it over with a little sack, & the juice of a lemon, then scrape on sugar, & serve it upon a plate.

This kind of dish, where leftover bread is soaked in eggs and cream and then fried in a pan, was popular all over Europe. This is a particularly good variation on the theme, which is flavored with rose water and sack. A slightly earlier French version suggests one scatters sugar over the finished dish and glaze it with a fire shovel.[11] A tansy was a kind of pancake flavored with the bitter herb tansy (*Tanacetum vulgare*). A manchet was a small white loaf that weighed about six ounces.

✦ MENU FOR AN AUTUMN OR WINTER TABLE

Of twelve covers, served with nine plates for each service, for dinner

First Service

For the middle: a small garnished surtout

Two soups
One of turnips
One of cardoons in broth

Six hors d'oeuvres
One of Provencal andouilletes
One of lamb rissoles
One of a balotine of pheasant
One of little green stuffed cabbages
One of grilled sheep tongues
One of little woodcock pates

Remove for the two soups
One of a Royal Hotchpotch
One of a leg of veal in stoffado

Second Service

Three little entrees
One of the family partridges
One of fillets of plovers a la Mancelle
One of fillets of chicken in a truffle cream sauce

Three other little entrees
One of little sheep breads in their juice
One of fried turkey wings with a puree of turnips
One of fillets of hare in their sauce

Third Service

Two cold entremets
One of a marbled galantine
One of a sausage pate

Four plates of roast meat
One of little baby birds
One of snipe
One of red partridges
One of little chickens a la Dauphine
Lemon and Orange

Two salads
One of wild chicory
One of lettuce[12]

❧ 54. AN AMULET OF ASPARAGUS ❧

England 1744. (Adam's Luxury, 116)

Cut and blanch your asparagus in small pieces, and fry them in butter with parsley and chibol. Then pour some cream over them, and having seasoned them, boil them. Then make an amulet of eggs, cream and salt; when it is enough dress it on a dish, and having thickened it with yolks of eggs, pour it on the amulet, and serve it.

An amulet is the eighteenth-century English name for an omelet. It is close to the earliest French name—*aumelette.* This omelet is an easy dish to prepare. The asparagus pieces are first gently fried with some chibol (green or spring onion) and parsley. They are then made into a fricassée with a little cream and cooked gently until they are soft. This is then used as the filling for an omelet.

⊰ 55. EGGS POACHED WITH ANCHOVIES ⊱

France 1737. (l'Ecole parfaite des officiers de bouche, 411)

Poach some eggs in water; once poached, take some anchovies, blend them on a plate with good fresh butter; next pass them through a sieve with fried flour, some lemon juice and a little salt, dish up your eggs, pour this sauce over them and serve them.

This dish initially appeared in 1662 in the first edition of *l'Escole parfaite*, alongside *Eggs à la Intrigue*, quoted at the beginning of this section. However, the original recipe contained nutmeg. By 1737, when this version of the recipe was published, the nutmeg was omitted. As new editions of old cookbooks were published in France, the original recipes were modified to cater for changing tastes. Some old fashioned ones, such as *Eggs à la Intrigue*, were completely omitted from these later editions.

SAUCES

⊰ 56. CAPON LIVER SAUCE ⊱

Italy 1662. (Stefani, 55)

Take twelve capon livers, fry them in butter, pound in a mortar, mix in a pinch of powder of cloves, a quarter of an ounce cinnamon, three ounces of sugar, a little nutmeg, and blend this mixture with a half glass of malvasia, two ounces of orange juice, pass through a sieve, heat it gently, because it does not have to cook much: serve it on roasted game.

This rich, strong-tasting sauce is typical of the sweet-sour sauces that were popular at this period for accompanying game. Malvasia is a sweet wine made from the prized Malvasia grape. If you want to try making this generously spiced sauce, use chicken livers and make sure the orange juice is from Seville oranges. If this is unavailable use lemon juice instead.

⊰ 57. JASMINE FLOWER SAUCE ⊱

Italy 1662. (Stefani, 55)

Take a pound of jasmine flowers, pound them in a mortar, with half an ounce of cinnamon, two mostaccioli di Napoli, dissolve in a pound of rose vinegar, and two ounces of sugar, bring this composition to the boil in a glazed ceramic vessel covered with paper, and a lid, give it a gentle cook, this sauce serves for roasted liver, fried steaks and other things.

Floral flavorings for savory meat dishes were an important feature of Italian cookery in this period. As well as elderflowers, roses, and citrus flowers, the heady perfume of jasmine was also popular. This very acidic sauce, which can be stored in a bottle for a long period, was thickened with Neapolitan mostaccioli, a kind of spice cake. If you want to try making some, see recipe 91.

⅋ 58. TOMATO SALSA SPANISH STYLE ⅋

Italy (Naples) 1692. (Latini, vol. 1, 444)

Take half a dozen tomatoes, that are mature; put them on the embers to sear, and after they are toasted, remove the skins with care, and mince them finely with the knife and add unto them finely chopped onion to your taste, chili pepper also cut small, chervil, or peppermint in small measure, and mix all these things together, season with a little salt, oil and vinegar, this makes a very tasty salsa for boiled meats and for other dishes.

Tomato sauces of this kind are typical of modern Italian cuisine. However, this particular recipe is the earliest one to be published in an Italian cookbook. It contains two New World ingredients, tomatoes and chili peppers, both introduced into Naples by the Spaniards who ruled the city during this period. Both these plants had been known in Italy for some time and were grown as ornamentals, but their culinary potential was only realized at the end of the seventeenth century.

SAVORY PIES AND PASTRIES

⅋ 59. A PORTUGUESE PIE ⅋

France 1656. (de Lune, 249)

Mince a breast of poulet d'Inde (turkey) with beef marrow, season with salt, pepper, cinnamon, garnish with citron peel, Levantine dates, chopped pistachios, prunes de Brignolle, currants, pounded bacon fat, and make a pie crust with puff paste in the form of two dolphins on a sheet of paper, making sure that both of them are joined along the back, having created this shape with your pastry and filled it with the meat, cover it with the same pastry, when almost baked, glaze it with sugar and orange flower water, then make a sweet-sour sauce with lemon juice and sugar, which you will pour in your pie, when serving, garnish with pomegranate kernels.

A design for a pie in the form of a dolphin.

The modern word *dindon* is a contraction of *poulet d'Inde,* which is the earliest French name for the turkey. This sweet-sour pie with its minced turkey, dates, dried fruit, and orange-flower flavoring is a typical product of a high-status pastry cook at this time. This old-fashioned dish had its origins in the late medieval and Renaissance kitchen and was destined to become obsolete as the advancing French culinary enlightenment encouraged a strong differentiation between the sweet and the savory. By the 1750s, recipes like this had disappeared from French cookbooks. Pastries in the shape of dolphins (the emblem of the dauphin) were popular and there are some striking illustrations to guide the culinary artist in their construction.

⇥ 60. TO MAKE A LUMBER PIE ⇤

England 1660. (May, 224)

Take some grated bread, and beef-suet cut into bits like great dice, and some cloves and mace, then some veal or capon minced small with beef suet, sweet herbs, fair sugar, the yolks of six eggs boil'd hard and cut in quarters, put them to the other ingredients, with some barberries, some yolks of raw eggs, and a little cream, work up all together and put it in the caul of veal like little sausages; then bake them in a dish, and being half baked have a pie made and dried in the oven; put these puddings into it with some butter, verjuice, sugar, some dates on them, large mace, grapes, or barberries, and marrow—being baked, serve it with a cut cover on it, and scrape sugar on it.

Lumber pies are very common in seventeenth- and early-eighteenth-century English cookbooks. They are always filled with little balls of meat or fish, usually cooked with sour fruit like barberries, gooseberries, or grapes. The word lumber is said to be derived from Lombard, signifying a northern Italian origin for this kind of pie. Similar pastries known as *pasticetti*, which were filled with veal *polpettine* (meatballs), were popular in some parts of Italy, so there could be some truth in this theory. As in the previous recipe, the pie filling is seasoned with sugar to give a sweet-sour flavor. The recipe tells readers to make a pie case and dry it in the oven. In England this kind of freestanding pie case was known as a coffin, in France as an *abbesse*, and in Italy as a *casa*—literally a house. A hot-water crust or strong rye pastry was the most suitable pastry for this purpose. See recipe 175 for directions to make a coffin of this kind. The pie was crowned with a decorative cut cover. These were often made of puff pastry in a complex latticework, allowing the diners to see the colorful filling through the lid.

⇥ 61. SMALL PIGEON PASTICCETTI ⇤

Italy 1692. (Latini, vol. 1, 345)

Having rolled out some puff pastry, form the pie case, and put in a plucked and cleaned pigeon, well separated from his bones, cut him into two or three pieces, remove the

Decorative pie designs.

head and the feet, you add his liver, little slices of soft bacon fat, slices of prosciutto, and of soppressata, little sticks cut from morels, when in season, or else small mushrooms, lemon juice, pine nuts, the usual spices, when it is to be cooked, sugar it on top, and give one to every one of your guests.

Line a four-inch pie tin with puff pastry and fill it with the breast fillets of the pigeon and any meat you can rescue from the bones, together with the bird's liver. Add some chopped bacon fat, some slices of Parma ham, and some pressed tongue (soppressata). Morels give an excellent flavor to these little pies, but use mushrooms if you cannot obtain them. In seventeenth-century Naples, the standard spices used for seasoning pies were cloves, pepper, and cinnamon. After you have squeezed in some lemon juice and added a few pine nuts, wet the edge of the pie case and cover with a puff pastry lid. Bake it in a fairly hot oven for about 50 minutes.

⇥ 62. GENOESE PASTIES ⇤

Austria 1719. (Hagger part 2, vol. 1, 23)

Roll out a sheet of ordinary pastry thinly, then with a metal tube or sugar-tin cut out rounds like a large communion wafer or host, twice as many as the number of pasties required, as each pasty uses two rounds. Brush half the rounds with beaten egg or water and place on each the appropriate amount of seasoned minced veal in the form of a small ball. Place the remaining rounds on top and press together neatly around the edges with the fingers and shape them as illustrated.... Bake in an oven or hot fat. Eat as a meal or use for decoration.

These little ornamental pastries were used to garnish the Green Soup in recipe 20. They can be made from any good savory short crust pastry. Fill them with the *gaudiveau* mix described in the next recipe. Cut the tops with designs.

⇥ 63. FRENCH GAUDIVEAU PIE ⇤

France 1737. (l'Ecole parfaite, 448)

Make a good gaudiveau with veal, beef marrow and fat, a little bacon fat seasoned with salt, pepper, fine herbs, chives and dress your pie in a good coffin, garnish it with mushrooms, veal kidneys, artichoke hearts, morels, andouilletes, it will take an hour and a half to cook, pour in a white sauce when you serve it.

Genoese pastry for garnishing soup (also see recipe 18).

A *gaudiveau* was a mixture of highly seasoned minced veal, fat, and herbs usually made in large quantities and kept at hand in a cool place. It had many uses in the early modern

French kitchen. Unlike the previous sweet-sour pies, this recipe is for an entirely savory meat pastry without sugar or acidic fruit. The anonymous *l'Escole parfaite des officiers de bouche* was first published in 1662. In the first edition of the book a slightly different version of this recipe is paired with another for a sweet gaudiveau pie in the Italian style. This sweet variant contains candied citron peel, dates, currants, lemon juice, and sugar. By the 1737 edition, the Italian gaudiveau pie was omitted, as are all the other meat pie recipes that call for fruit and sugar. By this time, French meat pies had become completely savory in character, with mushrooms, truffles, onions, and herbs replacing the fruit, sugar, and spices. Andouilletes are strongly seasoned sausages made from pigs' intestines.

❧ 64. ROYAL HARE IN A PIE ❧

Austria 1719. (Hagger part 3, vol. 1, 206)

In a deep-dish pie these are cut up rather small and browned in butter or bacon fat. Season well; add good minced sausage, potatoes and other small pieces of meat. Put into a pie crust of good short pastry with white stock.

Although this very simple recipe for a hare pie is very straightforward and cooked in a ceramic pie dish, the author gives some remarkable illustrations of free-standing, highly ornamented hare pies. The shapes of these were dictated by the form of the hare. Similar designs were published in England, but there are no French illustrations of this kind.

❧ 65. A MERMAID PIE ❧

England 1723. (Nott, M30)

Scald a Pig, bone it: then dry it well with a Cloth; season it with Salt, Pepper, and Nutmeg beaten and Shred Sage. Then take a couple of Neats Tongues boil'd, cold and dry'd, and cut them in long Slices, about the Thickness of half a Crown; then lay one Quarter of your Pig in your Pye, and lay slices of Tongue upon it; then lay on another Quarter, and more Tongue, and so on 'till you have put in all the four Quarters; then cover them with Slices of Bacon, and put in Butter and bake it; when tis bak'd, fill it up with fresh Butter. It is to be eaten cold.

By pig, the author means suckling pig, a piglet that was literally still at its mother's teat. Early modern diners had no scruples about eating very young animals because the meat is extremely tender. Throughout Europe, baby pigeons, juvenile rabbits, and very young geese were all considered delicacies. An earlier version of this pie was probably responsible

A design for a hare pie, 1719.

for its unusual name. Instead of the neat's tongue (a neat was a calf), the pig was layered with eel, so it was a pie containing both fish and mammalian meat—thus mermaid pie.[13] A half crown was a coin about an eighth of an inch thick. If you cannot get hold of a suckling pig, use pork tenderloin.

STARCHES, PASTA, AND LEGUMES

ঙ 66. RICE POLENTA ঙ

Italy 1662. (Stefani, 29)

Take two pounds of rice flour, twenty four glasses of milk, and half a pound of fresh butter, put the milk and the butter in a good clean pot on a gentle fire, be heedful as it is an easy thing for it to be spoilt by the smoke, when the milk comes to the boil, put in the flour, having first dissolved it in extra cold milk, it easily sticks like glue, and thus after it has been put in this pot, as it boils, mix it always with a stirring stick, stir continuously, whilst it becomes heated, when you see it is becoming hard, lift it off the fire, and with a silver ladle wetted first with milk, take little morsels of polenta, served on the plate with parmesan cheese, fresh butter, sprinkle with rosewater, and for every helping of polenta, put cheese, and butter, sprinkled with fine cinnamon; and when it is ready, serve straight away.

Polenta was originally made from millet or panic (a millet-like grain). As maize from the New World was increasingly cultivated, polenta made with cornmeal became more widespread in the Italian peninsula. However, before cornmeal polenta became the standard form, polenta was commonly made with rice flour. The method described here is very close to the modern method of making this important staple food, but the manner of serving with a sprinkling of cheese, rosewater, and cinnamon is very much in the style of the seventeenth century.

ঙ 67. SWEET CHICKPEAS WITH QUINCES ঙ

Spain 1662. (Montiño, 249)

Put the chick peas on to boil, and when they are done, take an equal quantity of quinces, peel them and remove the seeds, and cut them in half. Then cut the wide and the narrow parts of the quinces into thick slices. Take fresh cows'-milk butter and fry onion and quinces until soft, then add to the chick peas and season with all kinds of spices and cinnamon and a little vinegar. Add sugar so that the resultant dish is sweet and fairly dry.

Make some thick noodles and fry them, then place on a serving dish a layer of noodles (though the dish can be served without these), then another of chick peas, sugar and cinnamon, and in this way fill the serving dish.

Note that this dish has to be very sweet and very sour. If you have no good butter, use good oil, and if you have no quinces, make it with sharp pears.

Garbanzos, or chickpeas, were a very important staple food in the Iberian Peninsula at this time. In this unusual dish the garbanzos are served in a sweet-sour quince sauce.

❧ 68. RAVIOLI NUDI ❧

Italy 1694. (Latini, vol. 2, 140)

Take two pounds of ricotta, with four egg yolks and two whole eggs, and a little grated parmesan cheese, and six ounces of sugar; you form this composition into ravioli, you diligently cook them in boiling water, taking care that when they float to the top, then they are cooked; when they are ready, put them on the plate, with a little butter, with sugar and cinnamon on top.

Early recipes for ravioli often lack the outer casing of pasta to which we are accustomed today. We also tend to serve them with a savory sauce. In this recipe they are sweetened with sugar. Once you have incorporated the ingredients, make little balls by rolling them in a little flour. Cook them gently in a large saucepan of gently simmering water. Remove them with a skimmer as soon as they float on the surface and drain them in a colander. Serve them immediately with the dressing suggested.

❧ 69. GREEN STRUDEL OF SPINACH OR CABBAGE ❧

Austria 1719. (Hagger part 4, vol. 2, 31)

Take well-cleaned spinach, cook it, squeeze out thoroughly, take a handful of parsley, a handful of chervil, a little perchtram, some chives, chop all of these together finely, season with pepper and mace, add two or three spoonfuls of cream. Make a dough of fine flour and two eggs, not too thick, roll out into a sheet, as thin as you can, brush the sheet with melted butter, place the green mix on it and spread it to cover the whole sheet, then roll this over on to itself. Press with the back of a knife, to the size you want the strudel. Place in a boiling beef or pea soup, leave to boil as long as you would cook hard-boiled eggs, turn out on to a rack, place on a serving dish, sprinkle with breadcrumbs, pour over hot fat and serve warm.

In modern times we tend to think of a strudel as a baked pastry. This strudel is really a type of boiled pasta. The recipe contains an herb that was known in High German as *perchtram* and that was used in a lot of Hapsburg dishes. This was probably *Pyrethrum germanicum*, a flavoring we would find objectionable today as it is slightly toxic. If you want to try a close substitute, use chamomile. Strudels got their name from their rolled-up spiral form—in German *strudel* means a whirlpool. Roll out the pastry as thin as you can; traditionally you should be able to read a love letter through it! Cook the strudel in pea or beef soup for about five minutes. Although the author neglects to say, the strudel was sprinkled with fat and breadcrumbs and then toasted with a red-hot salamander or fire shovel. If you do not have one of these, brown it under the grill.

BREAD AND CAKES

⊰ 70. PUMPKIN BREAD ⊱

France 1654. (de Bonnefons, 14)

In order to make pumpkin bread, you need to parboil some pumpkin as though you wish to fry it, and pass it through a large cloth in order to remove the little strings that are left inside it, adding to it some water, in which the pumpkin has been cooked–as much as will be necessary to knead a dough in the usual way; and make your dough using two leavens in the same way as I stated before, you will make some very good bread, which will be a little rich once cooked and yellow, which is excellent for those who need some refreshment and who have an empty stomach.

This recipe first appeared in Nicholas de Bonnefons's book on gardening, *Le jardinier François* (1651), and later in a more complete form in his great classic on food and cookery, *Les delices de la campagne* (1654). The latter work includes an unusually detailed chapter on the bread-making processes of the period. This bright yellow loaf was almost certainly not one of the traditional bread recipes of France, but probably an invention of the author. In France, it was common to make bread with *levain* (what we would today call a sourdough starter), which is a small batch of dough that has been retained from a previous bread-making session and refreshed from time to time by feeding it with flour. If you make sourdough bread and keep a starter going, you will be familiar with the process. In the other bread recipe to which he refers, de Bonnefons explains how a levain is added to some flour to make the initial dough. The following day the dough is refreshed with some more levain to encourage it to go through a secondary rising process. This produces a bread of great character.

⊰ 71. AN EXCELLENT FRENCH BREAD ⊱

England 1677. (English receipt book)

Take half a peck of flour and as much new milk as will make it into dough, make it in dough with four eggs, whites and yolks well beaten, a pint of barm beaten with the eggs, put in the milk with a little salt, then make your dough and let it stand a little to rise covered with a warm woolen cloth, you must be sure to put them in as soon as they rise, and as soon as the dough is made make it in little loaves, then cover them with the cloth and as soon as they rise put them in the oven. Half an hour will bake them. Your milk must be warm.

Recipes for so-called French breads are common in seventeenth- and eighteenth-century English cookbooks. They probably evolved as a result of homespun attempts by English bakers and housewives to replicate brioche and other enriched types of white French bread. Although this is not as rich as a true brioche (see recipe 74), it makes a delicate and delicious white loaf. Barm was the yeast created in the beer-brewing process. If you know a home brewer, ask him to save some of the froth that forms on top of his fermenting ale and use it to raise your bread—it is extremely vigorous and effective. However, if your beer is strongly hopped, it can make the yeast bitter. A peck was a volumetric measurement equivalent to two gallons, so this recipe is for a gallon, or four quarts of flour. If you make it with a quart of flour, you will need one egg and enough warm milk to form the dough. If you use fresh baker's yeast, dissolve it first in a quarter pint of warm water. During the sixteenth century, a small loaf or manchet was made from eight ounces of dough, producing a loaf that weighed about six ounces. The manchet was still current in England in the 1670s, so if you make your loaves out of eight ounces of dough they should be authentic. Rolls and manchets were often slashed round the middle and pricked in the top before they were baked to encourage them to rise.

ᴈ 72. LADY STEVEN'S SAFFRON CAKE ᴇ

England 1677 (English receipt book)

Weigh four pound of flour and dry it well before the fire, then mix in it three quarters of a pound of sugar finely with mace, cinnamon and nutmeg to your taste, then rub in a pound and a half of fresh butter and a little salt. Then strain into these ingredients a pint and half of good barm. Strain it through a hair sieve with so much scalded cream as will do, to this put near half a pint of sack with half an ounce of saffron dried and rubbed, then infused in the sack over a soft fire, so pour it amongst the rest, then work them well together, not with kneading, but through your hands, then let it stand at the fire a quarter of an hour or half an hour, while the oven is heating, then put it into a hoop. It will take an hour and a half baking.

Large cakes of this kind were known in England as Great Cakes and were often baked in wooden hoops lined with paper. This unusual cake from Restoration England is flavored with saffron. If you want to make a smaller cake use half the quantities suggested in the recipe and bake it in a cake tin buttered and lined with greaseproof paper. However, the recipe uses an extravagant amount of saffron. A couple of small pinches would be enough. Dry the saffron in a cool oven for about six minutes and then rub it into a fine powder between your fingers. Dissolve it in the sherry (sack) that has been previously warmed and let it infuse for about 30 minutes. It will create a deep yellow liquid. If you cannot get hold of ale yeast or barm, dissolve some fresh baker's yeast in a little water and add it to enough cream to make the flour and other ingredients into a malleable paste. Add your saffron and sherry and stir the mixture together. Put it into your lined cake tin and allow it to rise. Bake in a medium oven for one hour. Test to see if the cake is cooked by inserting a skewer into it. If the skewer comes out clean, the cake is finished. If it is wet, cook it a little longer

⧫ 73. A CONE CAKE OR MOLDED CAKE ⧫

Austria 1719. (Hagger part 2, vol. 2, 38–39)

Put fine flour into a bowl according to the intended size of the cake, pour in warm cream or milk with a little white brewer's yeast and melted butter along with eggs as needed and the same quantity of egg yolks well beaten into the warm milk. Make the dough from this in the same way as for wasps' nests or pastry snails. Add a little sugar and a good amount of cinnamon, nutmeg and raisins, or omit the raisins if preferred. Put the dough in a warm place for a little while to rise. Heat the outside and bottom of the mould, pour in melted butter to warm and grease the inside, and when the dough is ready turn it out into the mould, but do not fill to the brim, as the cake must have room to rise nicely. Cover and heat from above and bake until done. When ready the cake is decorated with artichoke leaves made from sweet pastry and served.

Another Spit or Cone Cake,
Baked on a Spit

Make the dough as described above, but neither too fat nor too thin, and as soon as the dough has risen a little in the warmth, turn it out on to a clean table top or board and roll it in fine flour to the size required, according to the size of your spit. When the dough is rolled out, brush with melted butter, sprinkle it with a little sugar, cinnamon and nutmeg and if desired also finely chopped or coarsely grated almonds and raisins. Brush the spit with a little butter, wrap or wind the dough around it and tie it in a spiral from the top to the bottom with buttered string, though not too tight. Place by the fire and cook at a moderate rate, brushing with butter from time to time, and keep turning until the cake is well done and has a nice color, then remove it carefully from the spit and plug both holes until it cools.

These two Austrian cakes are made with the same dough recipe, but cooked in entirely different ways. The first is a kind of oven-baked *kugelhopf*, a light yeast-leavened sponge, which is still popular all over Central Europe. The second is roasted in front of the fire on a special spit and is much more unusual. The directions for making the dough in the first recipe are a little unclear, but if you want to make the molded cake, follow the method in recipe 140. If you are able to get hold of a spit with a wooden cone attached (they are still made in the south of France), grease the cone and tie some greaseproof paper round it with some string. Make much dryer dough than in the first recipe by using more flour and less cream. Roll this out on a floured board and then wrap it round the papered cone so that the two ends overlap. Cut straight down the cone with a sharp knife, but without cutting through the paper, and remove the excess dough. Wet the edges with a little water and join together. To ensure the cake does not fall off the spit in the early stages of cooking, tie it to the cone. Tape is better than string for this job.

Cone and spit cake designs, 1719.

◆ 74. BRIOCHE ◆

France 1746. (Menon, 269)

Put a litron of flour on the table and knead with a little hot water and little more than half an ounce of ale yeast; if you don't have any, you will add in its place a little piece of bread yeast. Wrap in a cloth and put it to rise in a warm place for a quarter of an hour in summer, and one hour in winter. Next, you will put two litrons of flour on the table with the paste, which you have made as the leaven, one pound and a half of butter, ten eggs, half a glass of water, nearly one ounce of fine salt, knead everything together with the flat of the hands, up to three times, sprinkle it with flour and wrap it in a cloth, in order to let it rise for nine or ten hours, cut the paste according to the size of your brioche which you wish to make, mould into rounds with your hand, flatten the top, gild with some beaten egg, bake them in the oven. For the little ones bake them half an hour, and the big ones an hour and a half.

Before the introduction of the decimal system during the French Revolution of 1789, bakers and cooks used an entirely different system of weights and measures. The *litron*, a volumetric unit for measuring dry materials like flour, was equivalent to 793.5 milliliters (a little under 3.5 cups, or 1.6 pints). In the eighteenth century, a brioche was not sweetened and was baked free standing, rather than in a mold. This recipe requires a sponge, or levain, to be made by mixing a litron of flour with some hot water and yeast and allowing this to rise. Another two litrons of flour are then put on a slab or worktop and a well is made in the center. Into this is put the risen sponge, the butter cut into small pieces, the beaten eggs, water, and salt. The ingredients are amalgamated by pushing them along the surface with the flat of the hand. If the mixture is too wet, more flour is added; if too dry, a little more water. It is kneaded like bread. Cover it and let it rise for about an hour and then knock it down and knead it again. Repeat this process three times. Then shape your brioches into round loaves. Flatten the top with your hand, glaze them with some beaten egg yolk, and bake them in a hot oven.

SWEET PASTRIES AND PUDDINGS

⇥ 75. A TORT OF RUBY RED WINE ⇤

France 1656. (de Lune, 287)

Take a half glass (demi-verre) of ruby red wine, a half cup (demi-tasse) of the juice of red currants, two macaroons, 4 egg yolks, and make it into a cream, season with sugar, the rasped rind of a candied lemon, a little salt, cinnamon, a small piece of butter, and put into a delicate pastry, garnish with orange flowers.

The *verre* (glass) and *tasse* (cup) were units of measurement that were frequently used in early French recipes. However, no standard definition of these has survived and they were probably rule-of-thumb measurements. This recipe works well if you use a standard modern wine glass half full of dark red wine and half a modern cup of juice pressed from some stewed red currants. Sweeten to your taste and add the other ingredients. Put the mixture into a short crust pastry case and cook in a gentle oven until the filling sets. Garnished with a few fresh orange flowers, this delicious open tort looks really spectacular.

⇥ 76. SWEET-SOUR TART ⇤

France 1656. (de Lune, 281)

Take a glass of verjuice or lemon juice, with four ounces of sugar, when it has boiled to half, put it to a pot of cream, six yolks of eggs, a little butter, orange flowers, grated candied lemon peel, a little powdered cinnamon. Bake it in fine tart pastry without a cover.

To make this delicious tart, you need to gently boil four ounces of sugar with a full wine glass of verjuice or lemon juice for about five minutes. Let this syrup cool, then mix it with a half pint of cream, six beaten egg yolks, an ounce of butter, a tablespoon of chopped candied peel, a few finely chopped orange flowers, and a pinch of powdered cinnamon. If you cannot obtain fresh orange flowers, add two teaspoons of orange flower water to the mixture. Line a tart tin with good short crust pastry and fill the case with the mixture. Bake in a moderate oven for about 35 minutes. Do not over cook, or the custard filling will curdle.

⊰ 77. TORT OF QUINCES ⊱

Italy (Mantua) 1662. (Stefani, 57)

Take six quinces that are not too mature, cook them in the embers, peel them with care, take the pulp and crush it in a mortar, take eight ounces of butter, six ounces of marzipan paste, a little cinnamon, a teaspoon of freshly ground pepper, a glass of cream, six ounces of sugar, a half pound of parmesan cheese, mix this all together, and have two sheets of puff pastry, take a tart pan of the right size, line it with one sheet of pastry, without anointing the pan with butter, put in the mixture, and cover with the other sheet of pastry with some ornament on top to your conceit, bake in the oven, serve cold with sugar on top.

Quinces were often roasted in the embers by wrapping them in a number of layers of paper. This works very well, but it is best to dampen the paper. If it is not practical to use this method, wrap the whole quinces in metal foil and put them in a cool oven until they are soft and thoroughly cooked. The time this takes will depend on the size and quality of the fruit. Do not use manufactured marzipan paste—it is far too sweet and artificially flavored. Make your own by kneading five ounces of ground almonds with three ounces of confectioner's sugar and a little orange flower water into a thick paste. The combination of quinces, almond paste, Parmesan, and pepper is unusual, but delicious.

⊰ 78. TORTA DI BOCCA DI DAMA ⊱

Italy (Mantua) 1662. (Stefani, 58)

Take a pound of marzipan paste, a pound of fresh butter, sixteen fresh hard egg yolks and eight raw, pound all in a mortar, beat for a while, that the mixture may rise, when ready mix in half an ounce of cinnamon, sprinkle a few times with citron flower water, when you know that it has risen enough, have ready a sheet of puff pastry in a pan, put in the composition, cover with another sheet, serve hot with sugar on top.

The Tart of the Lady's Mouth is a strange but romantic name for this frangipane tart. The ingredients listed are for a large tart. To make a smaller one, use half quantities. Make the marzipan as directed in the previous recipe. The filling is lightly aerated by beating the ingredients together. If citron flower water is unavailable use orange flower water.

⇌ 79. MEDLAR TORT ⇋

Italy (Mantua) 1662. (Stefani, 60)

Take three pounds of medlar pulp, a pound and a half of marzipan paste pounded in a mortar, add six ounces of butter, a little nutmeg, six ounces of grated cheese, six egg yolks, a pound of candied citron, or other candied fruit, provided that it is not Apples of Adam, because it might turn out too acidic, mix the composition well, make a sheet of puff pastry, and to ensure that it has the best scent and taste, put in some musk powder, butter the pan well, divide the pastry for above and below, fill it and cook it in a slow oven, serve hot with sugar above.

Medlars are the fruits of *Mespilus germanica*, a small tree belonging to the rose family. They are not edible until they are rotten. This is achieved by putting the gathered medlars into a basket or box and placing it in a dark place. After a while they go dark brown and soften, a process known as bletting. The pulp can then be squeezed from the fruits. It has a winey, applelike flavor and a mealy texture. This recipe is for a very large medlar tart. To make a smaller one, reduce the quantities by one third. Musk was much used in early modern cookery, but it is unethical to use it today. The tart is just as good without it. *Pomi d'Adamo* (Adam's Apple) was a variety of bitter orange.

⇌ 80. TO MAKE AN APPLE PUDDING ⇋

Netherlands 1669. (De verstandige kock, 17)

Take some golden apples, peeled and cut into pieces. Put them in a pan with water, Rhine wine and butter. Let it simmer, then mash thoroughly. Add half of its weight in white bread, five egg yolks, ginger and sugar. Mix everything. This is good.

This very simple Dutch apple pudding was probably finished by baking it in the oven in a ceramic pie dish. The same cookbook contains an interesting variation on the recipe that is worth trying. This substitutes grated gingerbread for the breadcrumbs and has the addition of powdered cloves, cinnamon, and pepper.

⇌ 81. TO MAKE LITTLE ALMOND, OR CHESTNUT, OR FILBERT PASTIES TO FRY ⇋

England 1677. (English receipt book)

Take a pound of almonds, or chestnuts, or filberts and blanch them and pound them with rosewater very small and put to them a pound of beef suet minced very small, the yolks of twelve eggs boiled hard and minced small, a pound of currants, mix altogether and put sugar and spice to them as you do mince pies, then make them into little pasties in puff paste and fry them.

These small fried sweet pasties are surprisingly light and delicious. You can choose which type of nut to use—the chestnut option is particularly good. This recipe is for making a very large number, so divide the quantities by four. Grind the nuts with a little rosewater in a mortar. Pound hardboiled egg yolks and suet together in the mortar with the ground nuts, add sugar to taste, then the currants, a half teaspoon of cinnamon, and a little nutmeg. To make the pasties, roll out a sheet of puff pastry. Cut rounds out of it with a three-inch pastry cutter. Put a teaspoon of the filling on the round, wet the edges of the pastry with water using a small brush, and fold it over to create a half-moon shaped pasty. Firmly seal the edges. If you want to be authentic, fry them in hot hog's lard. They only take a few minutes. Drain them on some kitchen paper. Serve them warm with a dusting of confectioner's sugar.

⇥ 82. A WHITE POT ⇤

England 1690s. (Rainbow manuscript, 40)

Take a pint of cream, boil it with a nutmeg cut in quarters, & whole mace put into it a quarter of a pound of sugar then take the crumb of a manchet cut in slices lay it in the bottom of a dish, with 2 handfuls of raisins of the sun stoned & sliced 9 or 10 dates sliced thin, half a nutmeg sliced & the marrow of 2 bones, put 5 or 6 yolks & 3 whites of eggs to your cream then pour it upon these things, and bake it half an hour.

White pots were the precursors of bread and butter puddings. By the crumb of a manchet, the author means the inside of a white loaf without any crust. Use about 10 ounces of sliced white bread to make this dish. Bake your white pot very gently as the cream will curdle if it gets too hot. Other recipes sometimes include a little rosewater as an additional flavoring. Remove the pieces of spice once the cream has been boiled.

⇥ 83. AN APPLE FLAN ⇤

Germany (Nuremburg) 1691. (Nürnbergisches koch-buch, 811)

Take Parsdorf Apples, cut them in half, remove the pips and core them. Fry the apples in fat until they turn brown. In a pastry flan case place toasted bread crumbs, chopped almonds, lemon peel, sugar and trisanet, or alternatively a solid almond filling. Place the apples on top of this until the flan case is full, then bake it. When it is beginning to set, pour on some good wine or malmsey, but not so much that it saturates the flan, and bake until done. When the flan is ready, lay pine nuts or chopped almonds on top of the apples in lines, about the width of the back of a knife, and slices of lemon and orange peel in bows or arches. The nuts or almonds can be toasted to taste. (It is not essential to fry the apples in fat. They can, if preferred, be lightly simmered in wine).

Parsdorf is a community near Munich, but this variety of apple seems to have become extinct. In its place, use a good cooking apple. *Trisanet* is also an ingredient that has disappeared from the German food cupboard. It once seems to have been an important seasoning, as it frequently turns up in medieval and early modern recipes from German-speaking nations. It was sometimes also called *trisenet* or *trisant* and is probably a foreign loan word from Old Provencal. It was a mixed spice powder. Here is a recipe:

> To make a small quantity of trisanet, mix 6 parts of powdered sugar, 2 parts of powdered ginger, 2 parts of powdered cinnamon, 2 parts of powdered mace and 1 part of powdered cardamom—store in a well-sealed jar.[14]

If you want to make the flan with the alternative "solid almond filling," use marzipan (see recipe 77). Malmsey is a type of Madeira wine. When you have baked the flan, arrange the nuts in a striped pattern over the filling, and then over the top of the nuts arrange the chopped candied peel in a series of arches or curves.

84. APPLE OR CHERRY DUMPLINGS

Austria 1719. (Hagger part 4, vol. 2, 26)

For these chop sour apples finely and fry until brown in fat. Add half the quantity of grated breadcrumbs with raisins, sugar, cinnamon and ginger, beat in as many eggs as necessary, form into dumplings, roll in flour and bake on a low heat in fat. Afterwards coat with a fine sauce (the dumplings can also be of cherries. If made from cherries and plums, the cherries must be sieved).

These substantial baked apple or cherry dumplings are a typical dish of the Austrian kitchen of this period. If you beat the eggs very well, it helps the dumplings to rise a little. The cherry option is very good.

85. BANNIET TORT

England 1730. (Carter, 119)

Take a Pint of Cream, and make it into Pancake Stuff; season it as you do Pancakes, and fry off eight of them fine, crisp, and brown; sheet a little Dish with Puff-paste, and lay in the Bottom, some Slices of Citron; lay on those a Pancake; then lay more Citron and Orangado, or Lemon-peel slic'd; then have some Sack, and Orange-flower Water and Sugar mingled together, and sprinkle over; Lay another; then more Sweetmeats, and sprinkle between every one still till you have laid them all: Lay Sweet-meats on the uppermost, and sprinkle what you have on the Top, and close it with a thin Lid, and bake it off pretty quick; and when bak'd, cut it open, squeeze in an Orange, and shake it together, and cut the Lid to garnish; sugar it over, and serve it.

Charles Carter was a very creative English cook who worked for a number of noblemen, including the Duke of Argyll. He had an eye for an unusual recipe and this remarkable pancake tart is one of his outstanding sweet dishes. You will need to make eight crepe-style pancakes first and allow them to cool. Line a tart pan a little wider than your crepes with puff pastry. Put a layer of chopped candied peel on the pastry base. Then build up a stack of pancakes in your tart, layering them with more candied peel, a sprinkling of sugar, sherry, and orange flower water between every pancake. Wet the edges of the tort case, put on a cover of puff pastry, crimp the edges to join the two sheets, and bake in a hot oven until the pastry is a golden brown. If you want to eat the tort in true eighteenth-century style, cut off the lid carefully and cut it into eight triangular shapes. Plant these vertically round the inside of the tart case to produce an effect like a crown. Squeeze the juice of a Seville orange or lemon over the pancakes.

☙ 86. PRUNELLA AND TAMARIND TORT ❧

England 1730. (Carter, 123)

First sheet a dish with puff paste, and lay your Prunellas or Tamarinds into the bottom of your Dish, two Rows of them; then boil up a Quart of Cream, and draw it up thick with the Yolks of ten eggs, some Sugar, a Stick of Cinnamon, and a Blade of Mace; fill up your dish with it over your Prunellas, bake it, and serve it, with a few Prunellas lay'd on the Top of it.

This is another of Charles Carter's remarkable pastry recipes. Prunella is an old name for a prune. Tamarinds are an acidic flavored seedpod much used in Eastern cooking. You can choose which fruit to use in this tort. Both options are excellent. If you use the prunes, remove the stones and arrange the fruit in the bottom of your tart case. If you decide to make the tort with tamarinds, you will need to remove the pulp from the pods and separate it from the hard seeds or buy some ready-prepared tamarind pulp. This sticky, dark brown paste is easier to handle if you rub some sugar on your hands and

Designs for torts and flans, 1719.

then roll the pulp into little balls, which you then put in the bottom of your tort case. The rest of the recipe is straightforward. Make custard with the eggs, cream, sugar, and spices and pour it over your fruit. Bake in a moderate oven until the custard has set and the pastry is golden brown.

Fruit, Nuts, and Flower Preserves

❧ 87. TO PERFUME APPLES ❧

England 1677. (English receipt book)

Take elder flowers and pick and dry them as you do rose leaves and when pippins are ripe wipe them and cover them with the elder all over and they will keep a quarter of year.

Apples were usually stored over winter in dry straw. This alternative method had a dual purpose. It not only helped the apples keep longer, but also perfumed them with the subtle scent of elderflowers. In Europe, the elder bush (*Sambucus nigra*) blossoms in the spring, while apples come into season in the autumn. The flowers would have been dried and stored until the apples were ready to harvest.

❧ 88. QUINCE COMPOTE ❧

Spain 1747. (de La Mata, 66)

Place the quinces, individually wrapped in paper, in embers; moistening the paper so that they do not burn, and leave to cook. So that they are evenly done all round, turn them from time to time. When they are done, remove the core and the skin, then place them to boil in a perol with clarified sugar and when they have absorbed the sugar and reduced to a jelly, they are ready to serve.

Compotes were an important feature of the dessert course. They were usually freshly prepared by gently poaching fruits of various kinds in syrup. Sometimes they were made from nuts, as in the next recipe. They could be served hot or cold. Clarified sugar was perfectly clear syrup made by dissolving the rough, rather gray cone sugar in water and boiling it with whipped egg whites and ground eggshells. These helped to remove the impurities when the syrup was passed through a jelly bag. A *perol* was a small cooking pot.

❧ 89. CHESTNUT COMPOTE ❧

Spain 1747. (de La Mata, 66)

Place the chestnuts prepared for the compote among embers, for in this way they will cook without burning, and when they are just done, rub them with the hand to remove the skins, then place in a saucepan with clarified sugar, and cook for a quarter of an hour. When they are soft, transfer them to the Compotero and squeeze over them the juice of a lemon. They can be served like this, hot, or can be boiled and then served cold.

Compotes were not preserves designed for storage. They were always freshly prepared and were served in a tall-stemmed serving dish called a *compotier,* called here in Spanish a *compotero.* Although this dish sounds rather like *marron glacé,* it is not so saturated with syrup and as a result is less cloying.

Sweets and Confections

⊰ 90. FRENCH FRITTER RECIPES ⊱

France 1656. (de Lune, 344–345)

Apricot Fritters

Make a batter with flour, yeast, milk and white wine, seasoned with salt, and when it is to a good consistency, neither too thin, nor too thick, leave it to rest a little, and coat dried preserved apricots with it, fry in clarified butter, serve with sugar and perfumed water.

Fritters of Prunes

Cut Prunes de Brignolle in half and make fritters with the same batter.

Fritters of Pomegranate Kernels

The fritters of pomegranate kernels are of the same paste as those made with red currants, enveloping them in the paste like the red currants, and take care with the cooking, making sure that they are well done, serve with musk sugar.

Leaves of Passience in Batter

Coat the leaves of passience in batter, and fry them in deep fat, serve them with sugar and perfumed water.

These recipes for fritters are a small selection from a number offered by Pierre de Lune in his important little cookbook. Fritters were popular early modern snack foods and were often sold cooked by street vendors. Passience leaves were obtained from Herb Patience (*Rumex alpina*), a plant cultivated in French gardens as a medicinal herb. This is a rare example of a culinary use. The leaves of sage and clary were also made into fritters in this way.

↝ 91. FINE MOSTACCIOLI ↜

Italy (Mantua) 1662. (Stefani, 77)

Take three pounds of blanched Ambrosian almonds, thoroughly wiped dry, grind very well in a mortar, sprinkle with citron flower water, mix in four ounces of powdered cinnamon, and two pounds of flour, be careful to mix it together a little at a time: take a pound and a half of clarified sugar, cooked to the long thread, put it in the aforementioned mortar and place all in a large ladle-shaped saucepan on a charcoal stove and with a spatula stir it, to ensure it does not stick; grind two grains of musk with a little sugar, put it in the said vessel, when the paste starts to turn to powder, then remove from the fire, when it is cool, form it into mostaccioli in the usual prints.

Naples was celebrated throughout Europe in this period for the quality and sophistication of its confectionery. The city was particularly famous for a wide range of fine biscuits. *Mostaccioli* were small, highly spiced cakes rather like gingerbread. Cinnamon was the chief spice used to flavor them, but some recipes included nutmeg, pepper, cloves, and candied citrus peels. Like gingerbread, they were printed in wooden molds. In other recipes, the mostaccioli dough was allowed to ferment for a few days before it was baked.[15] They were sometimes used as a base for making sauces (see recipe 57).

↝ 92. TO MAKE THE BEAN BREAD ↜

England 1670. (Wooley, 101)

Take a pound of the best Jordan almonds, blanch them in cold water, and slice them very thin with a wet Knife, then take a pound of double refined Sugar well beaten, and mix with your Almonds, then take the White of one Egg beaten with two spoonfuls of Rosewater; and as the Froth ariseth, cast it all over your Almonds with a Spoon, then mix them well together, and lay them upon Wafer sheets, upon flowered Plates, and shape them as you please with your knife and your fingers, then strew Caraway Comfits, and Oranges and Citron peel cut thin, or some Coriander Comfits, so set them into an Oven not too hot, and when they have stood about half an hour, raise them from their Plates, and mend what you find amiss before they be too dry, and set them into the Oven again, and when they are quite dry, break away the Wafers with your fingers, and then clip them neatly with a pair of Scizzers, and lay on some Gold-Leaf if you please.

These little rosewater-flavored almond cookies were very popular in seventeenth-century England. Recipes for them abound in both the manuscript and printed cookbooks of the period. They are easy to make, but if you want to make a lesser quantity, whip the white of one egg up first into a thick snow—then just use half of it if you want to use half a pound of almonds to half a pound of sugar. Use any kind of comfits you can obtain. If you want to gild the bean breads, use culinary-grade 24-carat gold. In some recipes they are called Bane Bread. A bane was a proclamation of marriage—we use the word *banns* today. It is possible that bean or bane bread was once a celebratory food associated with the public announcement of a forthcoming marriage. Make them on flat wafers or rice paper.

⋬ 93. SATIN BISCUIT ⋫

England 1677. (English receipt book)

Take five ounces of sugar finely beaten, two whites of egg. The sugar must be stroyed in by degrees into the eggs as you are beating them and you must beat them with a spoon a long time. The longer you beat them, the thicker they will be and the whiter. When they are so thick as they will lie in a heap without running thin, then put in a little caraway seeds. Then lay them on wafers about the bignes of halfe a crown and set them in a cold oven after tarts are drawn out and let them stand till the next morning. If you please you may put in a grain of musk or ambergrees.

There has been much discussion on the subject of the history and origins of the meringue. The first author to give a recipe for an egg white and sugar confection with this name was the French court cook Massialot in 1692. However, meringues were made well before this date, though they went under a variety of different names. The earliest known recipe is from an English manuscript recipe of 1604. This is slightly different from the classic meringue because the recipe includes a little flour. It was called "white bisket bread." The recipe cited here is also from a seventeenth-century manuscript source. Its evocative name, "satin biscuit," describes the whiteness and surface qualities of the meringue perfectly.

⋬ 94. PEPPER OR CINNAMON COOKIES ⋫

*Germany (Nuremburg) 1691. (*Nürnbergisches koch-buch, 867)

Beat well one fresh egg, stir in a quarter pound of well pounded and sifted sugar, the same quantity of fine flour, a whole ground nutmeg and two spoonfuls of cinnamon water or rose water. Stir the mixture well, then knead on a lightly floured board, roll out and cut out small cookies with a metal cutter, or shape them by hand if preferred. Lay them on a greased baking sheet and bake in the oven, but not too hard.

Spiced cookies and gingerbreads have always been an important feature of the German pastry tradition. The city of Nuremburg in particular has been celebrated for its *lebkuchen* (gingerbread) for many centuries. This recipe from late-seventeenth-century Nuremburg is for making small spiced cookies called *pfefferkuchen*—pepper cakes. They are flavored with grated nutmeg and cinnamon water. Distilled water of cinnamon is difficult to obtain nowadays. However, it can be replicated easily by adding five drops of essential oil of cinnamon to a half pint of water. Use it as you would rosewater.

⊰ 95. CHOCOLATE BISCUITS ⊱

Spain 1747. (de La Mata, 86)

Add a little grated chocolate to white of egg, sufficient in your judgment to give it its own flavor and color, and beat in a stone mortar. Add half the quantity of and shape you like, place on paper and bake in the oven on a low heat, applied from above and below.

These little chocolate puffs are really a kind of meringue. Similar recipes occur in cookbooks in French and English. Make the paste by mixing eight ounces of confectioner's sugar with two ounces of grated bitter chocolate and then turn it into a stiff paste with a little well-beaten egg white. Use a teaspoon to spoon small portions of the paste on to some rice paper. Bake the biscuits in a fairly cool oven until they puff up. Watch them carefully as they can burn easily.

⊰ 96. WHITE SPANISH TURRÓN ⊱

Spain 1747. (de La Mata, 99)

Having clarified half a pound of sugar and half a pound of virgin honey, the whitest and finest grade, all together, whip the whites of five eggs, incorporating them into the honey and sugar, so that one and another they reach the blown point, then stirring the whole until it caramelizes. When it reaches this state, pour in a pound of peeled almonds, finely chopped and dried on heat, and a quarteron of fine Holland sugar, broken into small lumps, and to add flavor, if you are in a hurry add some drops of a liquid flavoring or spirit, such as Aniseed etc. to the sugar lumps, but if you have time, rub the lumps one at a time against the peel of some strong-flavored fruit such as Florentine citron, Chinese orange, lemon, citron, etc. Finally stir all the ingredients vigorously with a spoon, then remove promptly from the heat, so that it does not pass the caramelizing point. Pour out at once on to white wafers, which must be laid out on the work surface on paper. On these the paste is spread with a spatula leaving it two or three fingers thick as required. Finally cut at once into pieces with firm strokes of a very sharp knife, and the turrón is ready to serve. It can also be kept if stored in a dry place.

Turrón is a kind of almond nougat that probably dates back to the time of the Andalusian Moors, though the earliest known recipe is from the sixteenth century. It is not difficult to make. Before creating sweetmeats of this kind, eighteenth-century confectioners had to clean their rather dirty sugar of impurities. They did this using the clarifying process (see recipe 88). Nowadays, it is not necessary to clarify the sugar, so just use ordinary granulated sugar. You will also need four ounces of sugar lumps broken up into small pieces for rubbing with citrus peel. A *quarteron* was about four ounces (120 grams). Blown sugar was syrup boiled to 240°F. Early confectioners determined that it had reached this temperature by dipping their skimmer into the hot syrup for a second and then blowing through the holes. If the molten sugar was dense enough to form large bubbles it was at the "blown" stage and ready for use.

Put the nuts into a cool oven to heat up—make sure they do not burn. Then put the honey into the saucepan and slowly heat it to evaporate any water it might contain. Add the sugar and stir with a wooden spoon. Whip up the egg whites until they are very stiff and stir them briskly into the mixture for about 10 minutes, making sure it is off the heat. Put it back on to a low heat and stir slowly until it starts to turn a pale brown. As soon as this happens, stir in the hot nuts and sugar pieces. Mix it well and allow it to cook for a few minutes more. Pour it onto sheets of rice paper and spread out to about an inch (two fingers) thick.

ICES

❧ 97. CREAMY SUNRISE SORBETTO ❧

Italy (Kingdom of Naples), c. 1690s. (Brieve e nuovo modo, 6)

To make ten cups of this sorbetto, take two carafes of milk, which you warm on the fire to blood heat. Put in half a rotolo of sugar, which you dissolve completely and strain it into the freezing pot. Then take an ounce of finely ground cinnamon, put it through a silk sieve and beat it into the milk with a large spoon, and put it into the snow. When it has half frozen, put in half an ounce of cinnamon water and three ounces of finely chopped candied pumpkin. If you want to make it in moulds, pyramids and cheese moulds, use three quarters of the amount of sugar. If you make it in moulds, in place of the candied pumpkin you can put in two ounces of pine nut comfits, when you stir it.

This remarkable recipe is from a small pamphlet on ices, published anonymously in Naples in the 1690s. Included among its 21 recipes are this one for the earliest recorded true dairy ice cream and also the first frozen dessert to be flavored with vanilla. Ices were made at this time by putting the ingredients in a pewter pot called a *sorbetierra*. This was plunged into a bucket filled with a mixture of compressed snow and salt, which caused the contents to freeze. During the freezing process, the *sorbetto* was stirred with a spatula to create a smooth, creamy ice. In Naples at this time a *caraffa* was equivalent to about 1.5 pints. A *rotolo* was just slightly under a pound. These proportions make a rather sweet ice for modern taste, so you might like to reduce the ratio to four ounces of sugar to the pint of milk. Preserved pumpkin can be bought in specialty Italian stores, but it is easy to make your own by storing cooked pumpkin in a bowl of dense sugar syrup. Keep this in the fridge. Pine nut comfits were sugarcoated pine nuts. Use the homemade cinnamon water described in recipe 94.

DRINKS

⊰ 98. RATAFIA OF QUINCES ⊱

France 1692. (Massialot, 391)

Take such quantity of the finest quinces that you can find; crush them and put the pulp in a strong sieve; press them together to extract the most juice than you can: this juice being well settled, you will add as many pints of eau-de-vie as you have quarts of juice, a handful of sugar to each quart, cinnamon, clove, of mace and coriander, in proportion to each other: having infused everything for some time, pass it through a straining bag and put it in bottles.

A *ratafia* was an alcoholic liqueur that was made by infusing fruit or other flavorings in alcohol. You will need access to a fruit press to make this extraordinary liqueur. Use it to extract the juice from some finely chopped quinces. Measure the quantity of juice you obtain and add to it half that quantity of brandy, marc, or *eau-de-vie*. If you cannot obtain any of these, vodka makes a good substitute. Sweeten it as directed and allow the whole spices listed in the recipe to infuse in the liquid for about a month in a sealed bottle. Strain it through a coffee filter and then bottle.

⊰ 99. WINE CHOCOLATE ⊱

England 1711. (Salmon, 105)

Take water, three quarters of a pint, choice red port, or rather choice sherry, half a pint; sugar chocolate a quarter of a pound, or something better; fine flour, or white starch, a quarter of an ounce, and a little salt; mix, dissolve and boil, and in about 12 minutes it will be done. But if you make it with chocolate without sugar, the proportion to the former water and wine, will be of chocolate, 2 ounces and a quarter, double refined sugar 3 ounces, fine flour or white starch, a quarter of an ounce, etc, as before.

By the middle of the seventeenth century, the new beverages of tea, coffee, and chocolate were becoming fashionable at the European courts. When this recipe was published in late Stuart England all three drinks were widely available to those who could afford them. The custom of drinking chocolate was introduced into Europe by the Spaniards, who had learned the practice from the indigenous peoples of Central America. This recipe is for a drink that is much richer than modern hot chocolate. Melt four ounces of a good-quality dark chocolate in the hot water and wine mixture and whip in half a teaspoon of cornstarch. If required, add extra sugar to sweeten it. The purpose of the starch is to prevent the chocolate butter from separating out. Whip it with a chocolate mill if you have one. Use a balloon whisk if you do not. In Spain at this time, an iced whip of chocolate called *Espuma de Chocolate* was popular in the summer months. This was introduced into Naples during the seventeenth century, where it was developed into a frozen sorbet called *scomiglia di Ciccolata*.[16]

⊰ 100. ROYAL USQUEBAUGH BY INFUSION ⊱

England 1737. (The Whole Duty of a Woman, 672)

You must take raisins stoned two pounds, figs sliced half a pound, cinnamon two ounces and a half, nutmegs one ounce, mace half an ounce, cloves half an ounce, liquorice three ounces, saffron half an ounce; bruise the spices, slice the liquorice, etc. and pull the saffron in pieces, and infuse them all in a gallon of the best brandy for seven or eight days, till the whole virtue be extracted from them; then filter them, putting thereto a quart of Canary wine, and half a dram of essence of ambergris, and 12 leaves of gold broken in pieces, which reserve for use.

Usquebaugh is the Irish word for *aqua-vitae* or water of life, from which the modern word whisky is derived. However, this unusual eighteenth-century liqueur is not really a whisky but a strong alcoholic drink known as a cordial, which was thought to gladden the heart and lift the spirits. One important ingredient of the drink is gold, a substance believed to have a strong beneficial effect on the heart. The words cordial and cardiac were originally related. It is easy enough to reduce the ingredients to make a smaller quantity. Ambergris (see glossary) is obtainable but very expensive—it is best omitted. Use 24-carat food-grade gold. Break it up into the smallest pieces you can.

3

🦅 THE REIGN OF LOUIS XV
TO THE FRENCH
REVOLUTION, 1750–1800

In the hundred years or so after the publication of François Pierre de La Varenne's influential cookbook in 1651, many dramatic changes took place in the French kitchen. By the middle of the eighteenth century, meat and fish dishes that combined sweet and sour flavors had become very old-fashioned. The mildly acidic condiment verjuice was still in use, but more rarely, and sugar had become a taboo ingredient in meat dishes. There was more emphasis on using herbs and mushrooms as seasonings rather than complex spice mixtures. Kitchens had also become much more organized. La Varenne's rational approach had now evolved into a full-fledged modular system. This enabled the chef to assemble a dish efficiently from stock ingredients already prepared by the specialists in his kitchen brigade. Never in the history of food has there ever been such an energetic desire to experiment with ingredients, techniques, and new ideas.

Since the late 1730s there had been a growing emphasis on simplicity, and the extravagant dishes of the early part of the century were now outmoded. These changes are evident in the recipes given in *Les soupers de la cour*, an anonymous four-volume cookbook published in 1755. This encyclopedic work was the last great French culinary text to be issued before the French Revolution of 1789. The culinary style described in its pages had a profound influence on the cuisine of other European countries. French food had become the cuisine of choice at all of the European royal courts, and the intricacies of French dining protocol dictated the presentation of food on high-status tables from Edinburgh to Moscow.

Despite the huge undertow of French gastronomic influence, cookbooks published in other European countries still extolled their own national food traditions. England was frequently at war with France during the eighteenth century and many Englishmen liked to think that their enemy's food was foppish and over elaborate when compared with the wholesome roast beef and plum pudding of the English squire. French food was therefore considered unpatriotic, so delicacies like the flavor enhancer coulis and ragoût were condemned as extravagant. Despite these protestations, recipes for these preparations were included in nearly every major English cookbook of the period. English female cooks were now selling many more copies of their cookbooks than their male counterparts. Authors like Hannah Glasse (1747), Martha Bradley (1758), and Elizabeth Raffald (1769) had fired the public imagination with their clear and well-articulated recipes. Unlike many male cooks who liked to show off with a flamboyant style of cooking, these women writers had an eye for economy and practicality.

In the Italian peninsula, some cookbook authors paid obeisance to the unstoppable triumph of French culinary progress. One anonymous Turin author wrote a work in 1766 called *Il cuoco Piemontese perfezionato a Parigi (The Piedmont Cook Perfected in Paris)*, which indicates how the new French ways were even coming to dominate the proud gastronomic traditions of Italy. However, the best Italian writers of the period only paid lip service to French influence, preferring to celebrate the characteristics of their own regional cuisines. One of the greatest food writers of this period was the Celestian monk Vincenzo Corrado, whose cookbook *Il cuoco galante* (1773) described the rich and imaginative food of Naples. He also wrote a book on confections, *Il credenziere di buon gusto* (1778), which devotes a whole chapter to ices, a fashionable specialty of this energetic and pleasure-loving city. One of Corrado's fellow Neapolitan cooks, Francesco Leonardi, earned the distinction of becoming the chef de cuisine to Catherine the Great of Russia. His six volume *l'Apicio moderno* (1790) was heavily influenced by French court cuisine, but it too contains many Neapolitan recipes. One of the most important developments in this period was the gradual takeover by the tomato of the role that verjuice grapes, bitter oranges, and gooseberries had held for centuries in the preparation of Italian meat and fish dishes.

In Spain, *Nuovo arte de cocina* (1745), by the Franciscan friar Juan Altamiras, became a best seller and was still being printed well into the following century. Altamiras was a professional cook who ran the kitchens of a religious school in Zaragoza. His remarkable recipes demonstrate that he was aware of the latest French developments, but these are never allowed to overshadow the delights of the simple food of his native Aragon. Portuguese cooking also remained distinctive and is well described in eighteenth-century editions of Domingos Rodrigues's *Arte de cozinha*. This work, the only cookbook in Portuguese until 1780, was first published in 1680 when

Rodrigues was cook to the royal Portuguese household under Pedro II, but its later editions were revised to keep pace with changing fashions.

The Revolution of 1789 brought about the complete restructuring of French society, which in turn led to some dramatic changes in food culture. France's imperial ambitions under Napoleon also had an important role in shaping new attitudes to dining. As a result of these cataclysmic events, cooks who had normally found employment with aristocratic families sought work in the kitchens of a newly fashionable outlet for fine food—the restaurant.

SOUPS

⍟ 101. GAME SOUP ⍟

France 1755. (Les soupers de la cour, vol. 1, 103)

Cut in pieces, either a partridge or a rabbit, sauté it with slices of veal, ham, onions, carrots and parsnips; let it brown a little on a slow fire; as you do for gravy; then add some good bouillon, according to the quantity you want to make; boil gently till the meat is done; strain the broth, and put it into your soup pot, and stew in it what vegetables you please.

The method used for making this rustic soup was one of the standard procedures of classic French cookery of this period. The pieces of game were fried with some veal and sliced vegetables on a charcoal stove. They were allowed to brown, and then some bouillon was added in which the meat was cooked until tender. Everything was then rubbed through a sieve, and the resulting purée was put into a large pan and the soup was refreshed with vegetables, which were cooked until just soft. Although no quantities are given, the recipe is written clearly and is easy to follow. It is representative of the much-simplified cuisine of the mid-eighteenth century.

⍟ 102. ORDINARY BOUILLON, OR MITONNAGE FOR SOUPS AND SAUCES ⍟

France 1758. (Marin, vol. 1, 2–3)

This bouillon should be made with every possible care. Take a quantity of meat as necessary. The best are slices of beef, beef rand and knuckle of beef. Add to this a chicken or knuckle or shin of veal. When it has been well skimmed, salt it lightly and add to it some suitable root vegetables, like turnip, carrots, parsnip, onions, celery and leeks, with some cloves and a root of parsley. This bouillon or "mitonnage" is used to cook everything which goes into the soups, like poultry, game, centre piece meat dishes, and all the vegetables, except for cabbages, radishes, large turnips and some other vegetables from which soup is made separately. The goodness of all bouillons depends on the amount of attention and care which is taken.

All French cooking authorities at this period insisted on making good-quality bouillon or stock from the best ingredients and with the utmost care. Bouillon or stock was the foundation ingredient of most other savory dishes and a stockpot was to be found simmering away in every kitchen. This bouillon is easy to make and can be used as a basis for not only the soups listed in this section, but many of the other savory dishes in this book.

⊰ 103. MINESTRA OF RICE AND CABBAGE ⊱

Italy (Le Marche) 1786. (Nebbia, 17)

You take the rice, and put it to soften in hot water for an hour, then take a cabbage that has first been cleaned, and then boiled in water with little salt; squeeze out the water well, and shred it fine, place it in a pot with an ounce and a half of butter, a little minced onion; cook them over the stove, and add a little sweet spice, a little salt, and abundant stock, so that the cabbage floats on this said stock; then put on the stove another pot with the same quantity of butter in it, put in the rice well drained, watching out that it does not stick, therefore you should be diligent to stir it well with a wooden skimmer, and refresh with stock until it becomes swollen, but not overcooked; then unite the rice with the cabbage; put in the pot three ounces of grated parmesan and incorporate it well, and in such manner carry it to the table. Soup with rice and celery is made in the same way as that of cabbage and rice.

This thick minestra is more like a risotto than a soup. The rice is first softened by soaking it in hot water for an hour, then thoroughly straining it and frying it in butter. Little by little some stock is added, in exactly the same way that a risotto is prepared today. When the rice is fully cooked it is incorporated into the cabbage soup, seasoned with grated Parmesan, and served to table.

⊰ 104. MINESTRA OF RICE AND TOMATOES ⊱

Italy (Le Marche) 1786. (Nebbia, 17)

Get ready the rice as described [in recipe 103], but prepare the tomatoes like this. Take the tomatoes and slice them in half, put in the pot with a little butter, an onion in slices and a slice of prosciutto, leave them to cook on a slow fire until they start to make their own sauce; then make the fire burn more lustily, and when the tomatoes start to stick, you put in some stock; keep it cooking in this way until it is almost time to send it to the table; then you take the rice, which you have prepared in the same way as for the cabbage soup, and put it in the tureen; pass the tomatoes through a sieve to make a good broth, and mix it with the rice, and send it to the table, which will be of good color and excellent taste.

This very simple tomato minestra is also a kind of risotto. A large slice of Parma ham or speck (bacon) contributes an excellent flavor to this robust country dish.

Meat

ᕗ 105. GARBURE ᕘ

France 1755. (Les soupers de la cour, vol. 1, 106)

Take a good piece of ham, slices of lard and beef, with two legs of a goose; let the meat fry a little until it has colored; then add bouillon, three or four onions, carrots, celery, and a green cabbage, first scalded in boiling water; boil it on a gentle fire until the meat is done; garnish the bottom of your serving dish with slices of bread, and soak it with some of the said broth until it browns; put upon it the ham and the legs of the goose; add only enough bouillon to keep it of a thick substance.

This traditional stew originated in the Midi-Pyrénées, where it is still prepared using an almost identical method. It was cooked very slowly in a *marmite* or *daubière* over the embers, often with hot coals on the lid. If you have access to a dutch oven, you could cook this hearty country stew in this authentic way. The lard referred to here is a piece of fat salt bacon, and not the rendered pork fat called by this name today. By goose legs, the author means *confit d'oie*, the traditional preserved goose of the South of France, which is made by cooking the goose in its own fat.

ᕗ 106. STOFFADO OF VEAL ᕘ

Spain 1758. (Altamiras, 41)

From the lean of the veal cut pieces the size of nuts. Heat some fat bacon and fry the veal pieces in the fat. Transfer the meat to the casserole, and in the remaining fat fry finely chopped onion and add to the meat. Add a little white wine, two crushed cloves of garlic, salt, all spices, parsley, and some bay leaves. After adding this recado, place on a low heat, covering the top of the pot with paper, so that it does not boil over, and covering this with a small pot containing water. Make up a little dough and place it as

Cooking a stoffado in the embers. The pot was sealed with a sheet of paper and a dish of cold water was placed on top.

a seal around the main casserole, so that the steam cannot escape. Leave to cook for two hours. In this way you will end up with a small amount of liquor, but of good quality and very tasty.

A sheet of paper is used to seal the top of the casserole, or pot, in which this stew is cooked. This is attached to the casserole with some sticky dough made with flour and hot water. A pot with a diameter slightly larger than that of the casserole is then placed on top. This is filled with cold water in order to encourage the steam to condense at the top of the pot and prevent the stoffado from boiling over. Altamiras uses the word *recado* throughout his recipes as a general term to describe various blends of seasonings and herbs. The word *stoffado* is derived from *stufa*, meaning stove—it usually refers to a stew cooked slowly on top of a stove.

⇥ 107. PORK SALPICOENS ⇤

Portugal 1765. (Rodrigues, 89)

Mince very well two arratels of lean ham and half an arratel of ham fat, and keep it for 12 hours in a marinade of wine, vinegar and a clove of chopped garlic. Make the salpicoen in cow intestines of the same size that you would make sausages; season well with chilli pepper and cardamom. Rinse the salpicoens in warm water and put them to dry. Fry them in butter and send them to the table.

These spicy cardamom sausages are easy to prepare. You will need to finely mince two parts of lean ham to one part of fat. Use Iberico ham and ham fat if you can get it. Do not add any salt to the mixture, as the ham will already be well seasoned. The sausage skins would originally have been filled with a funnel or a sausage forcer, a kind of syringe with a wooden plunger. Nowadays it is easier to use a sausage machine or a sausage extruder fitted to a food processor. Cow intestines are quite large. They are known today as ox casings and are readily available online from companies selling sausage-making equipment and materials (see appendix).

An *arratel* was a unit of measurement that was used in Lisbon until the nineteenth century. It was equivalent to 397.5 grams, or about 14 ounces.

⇥ 108. SUCKLING PIG STUFFED WITH MACARONI ⇤

Italy (Naples) 1786. (Corrado, 65)

Stuff the suckling pig with macaroni, first cooked in stock and well seasoned with cheese, pepper, chopped sausage, ham, and minced beef marrow and baste it with really good stock while it is roasting on the spit, or bake it in the oven, and serve it covered with an excellent coulis of ham.

Suckling pig has been popular in Italy since antiquity. To be true suckling pig, the animal must still be feeding on its mother's milk. The first-century Roman cookbook author Apicius gave 17 different recipes for preparing this most delicate of meats.[1] The Dominican monk and Neapolitan cookbook author Vincenzo Corrado also devoted a whole chapter to the animal, which he initiated by quoting a recipe from Apicius in which the suckling pig is boiled in stock and served with a sauce flavored with wine, honey, rue, long pepper, and coriander. The good monk obviously tried this ancient Roman recipe, because he declares it to be "an excellent dish." Corrado's other recipes include a French-inspired suckling pig fricassée, but are mainly from the local Neapolitan repertoire. In one distinctive dish, the pig is cooked over a charcoal stove and served with a sauce of quinces, cinnamon, and pistachios. In another, the suckling pig is stuffed with pieces of eel, fennel seeds, garlic, and bay leaves. However, nothing could be more quintessentially Neapolitan than the previous recipe, in which the belly of the pig is filled with pasta, sausage, and cheese.

POULTRY AND GAME

⪩ 109. CHICKENS IN PAPER CASES ⪨

France 1755. (Les soupers de la cour, vol. 2, 149)

Take roasted chickens and cut all the white meat into large fillets; marinate it about an hour, with a little oil, parsley, shallots, mushrooms, half a bay-leaf, pepper and salt; make cases of white paper, put the fillets in them with their marinade; and place them in an oven or under a brazing pan cover; when done, wipe off the fat as much as possible, and add a little coulis and a squeeze of lemon.

To make this dish you will need to make some little paper cases from cartridge paper. Since the chicken fillets used in this recipe are already roasted, they do not need a long cooking time, but the oven should be very hot in order to brown the surface of the meat. A brazing pan was a specialized saucepan with a deep concave lid that could be covered with hot coals. The paper cases would have been put on a stone or other fireproof surface and then the brazing pan lid would have been placed over them in order to grill the chicken. The finished dish was served in the paper cases.

⪩ 110. ROAST PARTRIDGES WITH SARDINES ⪨

Spain 1758. (Altamiras, 62)

After cleaning the partridges insert two sardines into the body of each one in such a way that they do not stick out. Roast the birds with a good coating of lard, or if you do not have this, melt some fat and pour it over the partridges, with some peeled tomatoes. To remove the skins, place the tomatoes on hot coals. If you do not have any tomatoes, pour over sour juice of limes or oranges, with ground pepper, salt and a little parsley. Roast between two fires and when the birds are done remove the sardines. When the partridges are served they will retain the flavor of the sardines.

In this eccentric dish the delicate flavor of wild partridges is infused with the distinctive oily savor of fresh sardines, an unlikely combination that might seem distasteful to modern palettes. However, the recipe is worth trying because the sardines contribute a subtle background note with a fugitive hint of the sea that does not overpower the partridges. The combination of fishy flavors with meat was much more common in the early modern period than it is today. The partridges were coated in a jacket or bard of pork fat, which prevented the lean partridge meat from drying up in the intense heat.

⊰ 111. DUCKS WITH QUINCES ⊱

Spain 1758. (Altamiras, 67)

Roast the ducks with a sauce of quinces. Peel these, halve them and slice them thinly, take fat bacon in cubes, fry this until cooked. When done, add finely chopped onion and sauté the quinces until soft. Season with spices and cinnamon; add a little wine, vinegar, sugar and stock. Take the ducks roasted with bacon, lay them on some slices of toasted bread, then pour over the sauce. This sauce also serves for other fatty birds, such as curlew and grouse, and for hare, and if you wish to dress a leg of mutton or a joint of beef, it is good with this sauce.

Quinces were just as popular in savory dishes in eighteenth-century Spain as they were in sweet puddings and confectionery. Their distinctive tart and honeylike flavor make an excellent foil for the unctuous texture of fatty birds like duck. This sweet-sour cinnamon sauce has its origins in medieval Moorish cuisine.

⊰ 112. PORTUGUESE PARTRIDGES ⊱

Portugal 1765. (Rodrigues, 61)

After the partridges have been gutted and cleaned, give them each six lengthways slashes; and put into the slashes the fat of ham, and close them up tight with a string tied round, put them to roast with fire below and on top in a deep pan, with oil, vinegar and chili pepper; after they are roasted, put them on a plate; leave some of the gravy to boil with a few capers; as it is boiling, pour it round the partridges and send it to table.

This distinctive partridge dish departs from traditional European methods of roasting this important game bird by including chili pepper in the sauce. Chili pepper was a New World spice that had become well established in the cuisine of the Iberian Peninsula by the eighteenth century. It was first described by the Spanish physician Diego Álvarez Chanca in 1492, who had encountered it on Christopher Columbus's second voyage to the Americas. The Portuguese, who learnt about chili and other capsicum peppers from the Spaniards, were instrumental in introducing the spice into Indian cuisine via their colony of Goa. The cooking method is really a form of brazing rather than true roasting, which always required a spit.

ᘓ 113. QUAILS ROASTED WITH PARMESAN ᘒ

Italy (Naples) 1786. (Corrado, 66)

Dress the quails with melted butter, lemon juice, salt and pepper, roast them on the spit, and baste them frequently with butter. When they are ready to serve, cover them with a crust made from grated bread and parmesan cheese, and dish them up with fried sage leaves around.

Another Way in the Style of the Farmer's Wife

Dress the quails in the way described above and put them on the spit to roast wrapped in fig or pumpkin leaves; when they are cooked serve with a relish of olives in oil.

These two brief recipes for roasting quails are typical of Corrado's unfussy approach. Compared with the often-complex instructions in French cookbooks of the period, his directions are simple but always imaginative. He wrote at a time when Italian gastronomy was dominated by French culinary fashions, elements of which he acknowledged and included in his books. However, he delighted in the simple, honest food of Naples and the Campania, and his work spearheaded the movement toward a new pride in Italian regional food. The first recipe here uses a technique known as *dredging*, where at the end of the roasting process the meat is dusted with a mixture of breadcrumbs and seasonings, in this case grated Parmesan cheese. The spit is allowed to revolve for a few more turns in front of the fire in order to brown this coating. Fried sage leaves were a popular garnish throughout Europe. They are fried in boiling fat for a few moments until crisp and then drained on some absorbent paper. The practice of wrapping small birds in leaves to protect them from the searing heat of the roasting fire is an ancient, though effective, way of keeping the meat moist and succulent.

ᵈᴴ 114. CHICKEN POLPETTE (MEATBALLS) ᴳ⁾

Italy (Naples) 1790. (Leonardi, vol. 4, 47)

Mince some chicken breast, or lean suckling veal, the quantity that you require for your polpette with a little pork fat that has been blanched in water or boiling stock, and the fat from around calf's kidneys, afterwards grind them in a mortar; then add some crumb of bread soaked in water of the same quantity in volume as the meat (squeeze it out well), grated parmesan, salt, ground pepper and nutmeg. Continue to grind; when it is a good paste, mix in a little chopped parsley, a little chopped marjoram, three or more raw egg yolks, and two whites beaten to snow. Form into little balls. Put on the fire a pot with a little white stock, when it comes to the boil put in the polpette, cook them gently. When they are ready, degrease, and thicken with a liaison of three egg yolks, whipped with a little cold stock, and lemon juice, and serve with a little of this sauce. Every breast of chicken requires two egg yolks, and one white beaten to snow. If you please, you can include in the mixture pinenuts, raisins and a little finely ground cinnamon, and cook it also a brown stock without making the egg and lemon sauce.

Various kinds of meatballs have been an important element of everyday cookery in the Italian peninsula since Roman times, though they have not always been called *polpette*. During the medieval period, they were normally referred to as *tomacelle*. In the Renaissance, the rather pretentious Latin name *omentum* was used by the humanist writer Platina to describe these ubiquitous dinnertime favorites, a name he found in the celebrated cookbook written by first-century Roman author Apicius. At the end of the eighteenth century, although the great Neapolitan cook Leonardi named his important six-volume work *l'Apicio moderno (The Modern Apicius)*, he had no such pretensions and called meatballs by their common Italian name. The incorporation of whipped egg whites at the end of the grinding process gives Leonardi's polpette a light mousse-like texture. Modern polpette are usually served with a tomato sauce. Leonardi's liaison of egg yolks, stock, and lemon juice is a much more subtle accompaniment that does not overpower the delicate flavor of the meatballs.

FISH AND SEAFOOD

ᵈᴴ 115. MACKERELS AS QUAILS ᴳ⁾

France 1755. (Les soupers de la cour, vol. 3, 184)

Cut one or two mackerels, each into three pieces; give them a few turns on the fire, with butter, chopped parsley, shallots, mushrooms, pepper, and salt; wrap up each piece in vine leaves, with a slice of bacon, and some of the seasoning; lay them separately on a baking dish, and pour the remainder of the seasoning into it, if any; bake them in the oven: when almost done, sprinkle bread crumbs over all; put it back to color; and serve altogether with a Champagne wine sauce.

This dish is best prepared with some fillets of mackerel that have been chopped into three pieces. Use very young, fresh vine leaves, or the kind that are preserved in brine to make *dolmades*, available from Greek and Middle Eastern delicatessens. The mackerel were said to resemble quail, because this small bird was sometimes roasted wrapped in vine, fig, or pumpkin leaves (see recipe 113). The sauce for this dish is made by deglazing the baking pot with some Champagne or other white wine.

☙ 116. LING FRIED WITH HONEY ❧

Spain 1758. (Altamiras, 85)

Having boiled the ling, remove it and set it to drain. Make the batter as follows: taking a little fine flour, for ten pieces of ling, add a bowl (escudilla) of honey and make a paste with a little water, then place the pan with a little oil on the fire and heat. This can be done any time you have to fry something, except on lean days (as mentioned in the section on meat dishes). Dip the fish pieces in the batter and fry. This is good for hearty eaters. You can also add eggs and saffron to the batter, but it does not have to contain honey.

Ling *(Molva molva)* is a member of the cod family and like cod it was commonly preserved by salting. It is likely that this recipe was designed to be made with salt ling. This had to be soaked in water overnight to remove excess salt and to re-hydrate the fish. If you cannot get salt or fresh ling, use fresh cod or *baccala* (salt cod). An *escudilla* was a soup bowl, but the word here is probably used to signify a small quantity. A couple of spoonfuls of honey added to the batter helps the fish fry to an attractive golden color, as the honey caramelizes in the boiling fat. This lovely color is further accentuated if you also follow the advice to include some saffron in the batter mix.

☙ 117. A DISH OF TROUT WITH LEAFY VEGETABLES ❧

Spain 1758. (Altamiras, 104)

Take some large trout, scale them, split them and cut into little pieces. Fry them in lean and fat bacon. Take some white lettuce hearts, which are the best, and cook them in salted water. When the trout are fried, fry some slices of white bread, then add the lettuce to the pan with the remaining fat and fry them so that they do not dry out. Remove them and place them on a layer of bread slices, then another of hearts of cabbage, then pieces of trout, then add pepper and oranges, and in the middle, pieces of the fried bread, and a few pieces of lean bacon among the cabbage, then more trout. Serve hot. To make this dish even tastier, use dripping instead of oil. But I can already hear your qualm of conscience, which goes something like this: Brother Cook, here you are dealing with fish dishes, in which bacon is forbidden, so how can we legitimately use dripping and bacon?

This little scruple, which, not being observed, would be a source of great pleasure to you, I wish to overcome as follows:

It is true that in this chapter it is my intention to cover fish dishes, and so I am dealing with trout, which by their nature may be eaten on days of abstinence from meat, but the method of preparing them described above is normally used on non-fasting days, and so this is something with which you cannot burden my conscience, for although I am a cook, I cannot allow you this pleasure, although it costs so little, because the pleasure and expense given by this poor cook are very much in conformity with Gospel teaching, as you will observe.

Juan Altamiras was a pseudonym for a Franciscan monk whose real name was Friar Raimundo Gómez. He was born at the end of the seventeenth century and died in 1769. Gomez ran the kitchens of a large religious school in the city of Zaragoza in Aragon in northern Spain. His recipes are often sprinkled with wit and dry humor, as in these idiosyncratic instructions for cooking trout with bacon and meat dripping. He anticipates that some of his more pious readers would see this cooking method as being against the strict dietary regulations of the Catholic Church, so he makes a little joke about it at his own expense. Of course the dish is designed for a day when meat was allowed and the bacon is an excellent addition.

⌐8 118. TO SCALLOP OYSTERS THE NICE WAY ℮

England 1760. (Bradley, 182)

Rub to crumbs a good quantity of bread in a clean napkin, let this lie ready; set a gridiron at a good distance over a strong and clear fire; open a parcel of fine oysters, set them up into scallop shells, and, when they are sufficiently filled, set them on the Gridiron and let them stew of themselves till they are pretty well done, then cover them with crumbs of bread and set them before the fire in a tin oven; turn them at times, and baste them with butter. Let them stand thus till the bread is thoroughly brown.

The term "a parcel of oysters" means a portion or serving. Two common items of kitchen equipment were needed to cook this dish—a gridiron and a reflector oven (tin oven). Both were used for broiling—the gridiron over the coals and the tin oven in front of the fire grate. This simple but elegant gratin of oysters was a popular dish in Georgian England.

❧ 119. RAGÙ OF CRAYFISH ❧

Italy (Kingdom of Naples) 1790. (Leonardi, vol. 4, 9)

Cook the quantity of crayfish that you require for the ragù, with a little water, salt, half an onion sliced, stems of parsley, a few bay leaves, a clove of garlic. When they are cooked, peel them, that is to say remove the little legs, pull the ends from the large claws, and the muzzle, remove the outer shell and peel the tail. Take a little white Italian sauce; or put in a pot some veal, some ham, some carrots, some bread, some parsley roots, some celery– all cut into dice, a clove of garlic, two scallions, a piece of butter, two cloves; pass all over the fire; when it begins to get dry, put in a pinch of flour, wet with good white stock, half a glass of white wine reduced to half, season with a little salt, crushed pepper, and let it simmer gently; when all is cooked, degrease, pass through a strainer or sieve. Thoroughly grind in a mortar the well drained shells and claws of the crayfish, grind in the said culì and pass again through a strainer or sieve; put this sauce in a pan, add the crayfish tails in a discreet quantity, keep scalding hot in a bain marie, or over the embers warm without boiling, ensure that there is not to much sauce, and it is delicately seasoned with salt.

During the course of the eighteenth century, Italian cookbooks became heavily influenced by French cuisine and the word *ragoût* was borrowed and Italianized into *ragù*. Nowadays, an Italian ragù is normally understood as a pasta sauce in which meat has been slowly stewed with tomatoes, such as the famous ragù napoletano. In the eighteenth century, there were many more varieties of ragù than are now found in Italian cuisine. Leonardi offers over 70 recipes, none of which contain tomatoes or resemble the modern Neapolitan pasta sauce in any way. Many of them are straightforward translations of French ragoût recipes. Others are for homely native Italian stews prepared from such vegetables as broad beans, cardoons, and immature artichokes. The previous recipe is for a grand courtly dish and shows the extent to which aristocratic French food culture had made inroads into the Italian kitchen. Leonardi adapted it from a similar recipe that had been published in the French court cookbook, *Les soupers de la cour*, in 1755. The pinnacle of his career was cooking for Catherine the Great and this is just the sort of noble dish he may have prepared for the Empress. It was made with freshwater crayfish.

SAVORY PASTRIES

❧ 120. MUSHROOMS IN CANELLONS ❧

France 1755. (Les soupers de la cour, vol. 4, 178)

Chop some mushrooms in dice, and put them into a stew-pan, with chopped parsley, shallots, chives, and a good quantity of butter; let it brown a little, then add some good bouillon, pepper and salt; simmer until the mushrooms are done, and the sauce much reduced; beat up three yolks of eggs with cream to make a pretty strong liaison, and add a lemon squeeze; let it cool, and prepare some good puff pastry, rolled pretty thin, and cut into pieces, rather longer than wide, to roll the ragoût in, in the form of a short thick sausage; wet the borders with water, to make the pastry stick together, and fry it to a good brown color.

Puff pastry was frequently deep fried at this time. When carried out with care and well drained afterward, it can be very light and not at all greasy. The word *canellon* crops up a lot in French culinary literature—it means "a little cane or tube," thus the well-known modern Italian pasta dish cannelloni. These little tubes of puff pastry with their filling of rich mushroom ragoût are excellent. Do not overfill the pastry, and ensure that all the edges are thoroughly sealed. These were probably used as a garnish for a stew.

⇥ 121. A CHESHIRE PORK PIE ⇤

England 1760. (Bradley, vol. 1, 56)

Choose a fine loin of pork, cut it into steaks, and take off the skin; pare a parcel of good apples, and having taken out the cores cut them into slices: These things being ready, make a good crust, and line a dish of a proper size with it; grate some nutmeg, mix with this some pepper and salt, and with this season the steaks well; lay in a layer of them first, then put over them a layer of apples, and sprinkle over these some powdered loaf sugar, cover this with another layer of the pork steaks seasoned as on the first, and then pour in a pint of strong white wine; put in a little butter at the top, then put on the crust, and send it to the oven with the orders that it be well and carefully baked.

This very English pie is filled with alternating layers of pork and apple. It is strongly seasoned with salt, pepper, and a little nutmeg. To achieve a sweet-sour effect, a little powdered sugar is sprinkled over each layer before the meat and apples are covered in white wine. Its name indicates that it may have originated in Cheshire in northwest England. A humbler Cheshire Pork Pie, designed for consumption at sea, was made with salt-pork and potatoes and lacked the wine. A recipe for this naval version was published by the celebrated cookbook author Hannah Glasse. It was included in a chapter of dishes entitled "For Captains of Ships" in her important book *The Art of Cookery Made Plain and Easy*, published in London in 1747.

✦ FEB. 24TH, 1763—THE CONTENTS OF A PYE LATELY MADE AT LOWTHER HALL

2 Geese	1 Curlew
4 Tame ducks	46 Yellow Hammers
2 Turkeys	15 Sparrows
4 Fowls	2 Chaffinches
1 Wild Goose	2 Larks
6 Wild Ducks	3 Thrushes
3 Teals	1 Fieldfare
2 Starlings	6 Pidgeons
12 Partridges	4 Blackbirds
15 Woodcocks	20 Rabbits
2 Guinea Cocks	1 Leg of Veal
3 Snipes	Half a Ham
6 Plovers	3 Bushels of Flower
3 Water Hens	2 Stone of Butter
6 Widgeons	The Pye weighed 22 stone[2]

⚜ 122. TUNA EMPADA ⚜

Portugal 1765. (Rodrigues, 135)

After marinating two portions of fresh tuna for two hours in wine, vinegar and garlic, put them to bake in an oven in a pan with a little of the marinade and a splash of olive oil; when it is half cooked, season with black adubos and lemon juice; make a pastry case, putting in the tuna with some of the marinade, put it in the oven to bake, then send it to the table. This is how you make your black adubos seasoning– cloves, cinnamon and pepper.

Shallow tuna pies, or *empadas d'atum*, of this kind are still made in Portugal and in the neighboring Spanish region of Galicia, where they are called *empanadas*. All families and bakers have their own recipes. In Portugal, empanadas are associated with Christmas festivities. Modern empadas are sometimes made with a crust that contains a little yeast. To make this early recipe, just use a good savory short crust. Divide this pastry into two, with one part slightly larger than the other. The largest portion is for the base of the empada, the smallest for the lid. Make the filling according to the recipe and allow it to cool. Roll out the large piece of pastry into a circle and put it on a lightly oiled baking tray. Arrange the marinated fish in the center, spreading it out evenly to a little less than an inch high. Leave a border of pastry free of the fish filling all around, to a width of about one and a half inches. Brush this border with a little water. Roll the smaller portion of pastry to just slightly wider than the width of the filling and carefully position this over the fish. Fold the border of the lower pastry circle over the top one and join the two, pressing all around with a fork or pastry crimper. In modern Portuguese, the word *adubos* means compost or fertilizer—in the cookbooks of the eighteenth century it was a mixture of spices and flavorings.

⊰ 123. TIMBALO OF MACARONI ⊱

Italy 1786. (Corrado, 164)

The pastry for a timbalo can be puff pastry or short pastry, but without sugar. Cook the macaroni in beef stock, drain it dry and allow it to cool, you then enrich the pasta with a quantity of thick beef sauce, with pork sausages, mushrooms, truffles and ham, which if you prefer can all be finely chopped and cooked in the said sauce. Encase all in the pastry and bake it in the oven, and serve it.

This celebrated aristocratic dish is usually associated with southern Italy, though it appears to have been popular throughout Italy. The word *timbalo* is derived from the French *timbale,* which was a cylindrical food mold made of copper. However, to make this extraordinary macaroni pie today, all you need is a greased round cake tin, preferably one with a removable base. Carefully line it with thinly rolled short or puff pastry so that a little pastry is left overhanging the rim of the tin, reserving enough of the pastry to make a lid. Make your macaroni filling by blending some cooked short macaroni with a rich, highly seasoned beef sauce in which you have cooked some pieces of salami, mushrooms, prosciutto, and truffles (if you can obtain them). If truffles are beyond your budget, a few drops of good-quality truffle oil will provide an authentic flavor. When your macaroni has completely cooled, use it to fill your timbalo. Brush the top of the pastry with a little cold water and cover with the lid. Trim off the excess and crimp the pastry together. Bake it at a fairly high temperature and when the pastry has set crisp, carefully turn it out of the mold. Brush it with beaten egg yolk and sprinkle with grated Parmesan cheese and put it back in the oven until it turns a lovely golden color.

STARCHES AND PASTAS

⊰ 124. LASAGNA WITH ANCHOVY SAUCE ⊱

Italy (Le Marche) 1786. (Nebbia, 166)

Make the lasagne, take anchovies, or sardines, of excellent quality, wash, and thoroughly clean them well of their scales, head and bones. Take a cooking pot with oil, place on a stove, and boil in it a little flour; cook it until it comes to the color of cinnamon, mince garlic, as you please, herbs and marjoram, and the anchovies minced, fry together and incorporate, serve a large ladle of lasagne cooked in stock and drizzle with this sauce and sweet spices, and serve to table.

This is not a baked lasagna dish of the kind so commonly made today. Instead the sheets of lasagna are cooked in stock and then dressed with a pungent anchovy and garlic sauce. The author explains in a previous recipe how the lasagna were prepared by rolling freshly made egg pasta out into thin sheets. By sweet spices were meant cinnamon and nutmeg. Nebbia gives recipes for a few other lasagna dishes—one is flavored with truffles and Parmesan, another with walnut sauce, and a third with chocolate!

⊰ 125. MACARONI AL FIOR DI LATTE ⊱

Italy (Kingdom of Naples) 1790. (Leonardi, vol. 3, 285)

When the macaroni has been cooked in salted water drain it; take a pot and put a piece of butter in it, put in the macaroni, pass it over the fire, for every pound of macaroni add a half foglietta of heavy cream, a little salt, ground pepper, and nutmeg; stir well over the fire; remove from the heat, put in some grated parmesan cheese in proportion, mix well, pour into an earthenware terrine, cover with parmesan, sprinkle with melted butter; cook it to a good colour in a very hot oven, and serve immediately.

In seventeenth century Naples, pasta was usually served sprinkled with cinnamon and sugar, but by the end of the eighteenth century it was more usually eaten as a savory dish. This recipe is for a rich version of what we would call today macaroni and cheese. Macaroni and other types of pasta were the most important staple foods in Naples at this period—indeed, it was known as the city of macaroni eaters. To feed the enormous demand, dried pasta was produced on an industrial scale in the nearby towns of Torre Annunziata and Castellammare di Stabia. It was also served cooked in a veal or beef stock and sprinkled with Parmesan, a dish Leonardi calls *Macaroni alla Napoletana*. In modern Italy, *fior di latte* is a name for a type of mozzarella cheese. When this recipe was written it meant thick cream—literally "the flower of the milk." A *foglietta* was a liquid measure equivalent to about 456 milliliters, so a half *foglietta* was just slightly less than half a pint.

⊰ 126. SARTÙ OF RICE ALLA SULTANA ⊱

Italy (Kingdom of Naples) 1790. (Leonardi, vol. 3, 309)

Take a pound and a half of rice and wash it well in lukewarm water, put it in a well cleaned pot, with three ounces of minced beef marrow rubbed through a sieve, cook over a gentle fire for half a quarter of an hour, then add to it little by little a well flavored broth, season with salt, crushed pepper and nutmeg, cook for about forty minutes until it is very dry. When you have cooked the rice as described, withdraw it from the fire, put in eight or ten raw egg yolks, and mix these in well while it is warm. When it has cooled add three handfuls of grated parmesan cheese, and stir it again. Take the dish on which you are going to serve your sartù, and erect on it with the rice the sartù in the form of a pie filled with a good ragù of your choice. Gild the entire outside with beaten egg yolk, and sprinkle it with grated parmesan. Then let it take a very nice golden color in a very hot oven, and serve with a little truffle coulis round the rim of the plate and poured over the sartù. If you want to make it in a copper mold, grease this with butter, line it with the rice while it is hot, paying attention to press the rice into all of the angles of the mold, put the ragù into the middle, cover with the rest of the rice, smooth over with a knife, allow it to cool and dip the mold in boiling water, turn it out on to the plate on which it is to be served, positioning it exactly in the centre, gild with beaten egg, sprinkle with grated parmesan, let it take a good color in a very hot oven, and serve with a little coulis poured round the rim of the plate.

This ambitious recipe is a forerunner of the modern Neapolitan *sartù di riso*, a baked rice dish filled with layers of various cheeses, salami, and ham. It is usually served on Christmas Eve. The *sartù* was a close relative of the timballo and the pupton, recipes for which can also be found in this book. Leonardi mentions two methods for making the *sartù*. The first and most difficult is to form the rice paste into the shape of a freestanding pie. To achieve this, you need to mold the prepared rice in your hands into a perfect cone shape. Do this on a sheet of greased paper on a baking tray. Remove the top third of the cone for the lid. Then using your fingers make a hollow in the cone of rice and shape it in the same way that you would make a pot out of clay. If you rotate the paper as you do this, you will find it will help you produce an even shaped *sartù*. However, it does take a lot of practice to get a perfect result. Fill the *sartù* case three quarters full with a ragoût of your choice (see recipes 23, 47, and 119). Make a cover with the rest of the rice mixture.

To make the *sartù* using Leonardi's second method you will need access to a large *kougelhopf* or Turk's cap mold. This must be thoroughly greased with plenty of butter. Push half the rice mixture around the walls of the mold to make an even lining. Fill it three quarters full with your precooked filling and then use the rest of the rice to seal it in. It helps to put the mold in a cool place to allow the rice to set firm. You do not cook the *sartù* in the mold. Remove the *sartù* by dipping the mold in very hot water. It should drop out easily onto a baking tray. Whichever way you choose to make the *sartù*, make sure you brush it with egg yolk and sprinkle it with grated Parmesan cheese before coloring it in a hot oven.

⊰ 127. A POTATO PUDDING TO BE FIRED BELOW MEAT ⊱

Scotland 1795. (Frazer, 169)

*Boil and skin half as many potatoes as will fill your dish; beat them, and mix
in some sweet milk; put them on the fire with a good piece of butter; season
them properly with salt, spices, and an onion shred small; put it into a dish,
and fire it below a roast of beef or mutton until it is of a fine brown; if you
choose, cast three eggs well and mix it with the potatoes before they go into
the dish, to make them rise and eat light. Pour off all of the fat that drops from
the meat before you send it to the table.*

By the eighteenth century, British cooks had become the acknowledged
masters of roasting meat to perfection in front of an open fire. While the
joint was rotating on a spit in front the roasting range, it was common
practice to toast or "fire" a pudding underneath in the dripping pan. The
most famous of these was Yorkshire pudding. Another commonly made in
Scotland at this time and based on potatoes is described in this recipe. To
make this to best effect it really does need to be cooked under a joint of meat
in front of a hot fire, but it is possible to cook it in an oven if you place your
joint on a trivet to allow the juices to drip on to the pudding. Season your
potato mixture well with plenty of pepper, salt and nutmeg. The gravy that
drips onto the surface of the pudding browns in the heat and creates a highly
flavored crust. Although the dish accumulates quite a lot of fat on top of the
pudding, this is necessary as it fries the surface of the pudding. It is easily
poured off when the pudding is ready for the table.

Most early cookbooks give examples of menus. These are usually for
grand special occasions and give little clues as to the nature of ordinary
everyday meals. An exception to this is Charlotte Mason's The *Lady's
Assistant* (London, 1773), which lists dozens of family menus like the
two here.

Family Dinners of Five Dishes

Gravy Soup
Pork Roasted
Apple Sauce and Melted Butter
Potatoes
Baked Bread Pudding

Mackarel
Shoulder of Lamb Roasted
Fennel Sauce and Apple Sauce
French Beans
Ground Rice Pudding

Eggs and Dairy

⇥ 128. EGGS IN PAPER CASES ⇤

France 1755. (Les soupers de la cour, vol. 4, 84)

Mix some chopped sweet herbs, with a bit of butter, pepper and salt; put a little of this farce into the bottom of each paper case, break an egg into each case, lay some more of the farce upon the eggs, and strew bread crumbs over; broil over a gentle fire, and colour the top with a hot shovel; they must be as soft as if boiled in the shells.

This is a novel and very effective way of cooking eggs. You will first need to make some small paper cases—one for each egg. Cover the bottom of the cases with the herb and butter mix. Thyme, savory, marjoram, parsley, and tarragon are all excellent for this purpose. Carefully break in your eggs. Gently cover with more of the herb butter and sprinkle with breadcrumbs. If you have one, place the cases on a gridiron and cook the eggs over a gentle barbecue. Finish them off under a broiler, or use a red-hot salamander, or fire shovel, as suggested in the recipe. The breadcrumbs should be golden brown. Serve the eggs in their paper cases.

⇥ 129. OUEFS AU PRESIDENT ⇤

France 1755. (Les soupers de la cour, vol. 4, 95)

Dip well-drained poached eggs in beaten yolks, strew over them grated parmesan cheese and bread crumbs; fry for a moment in very hot boiling fat; serve with fried parsley.

This is an ingenious and effective way of serving eggs, but it does require a delicate hand. Mix some grated Parmesan cheese with some bread-crumbs—about two parts of breadcrumbs to one part of cheese. Poach the eggs very carefully and when they are firm enough to handle remove them from the water with a strainer. Let them drain for a few moments, and when they are cool, coat them thoroughly with beaten egg yolk. Carefully place them one at a time onto the breadcrumb and cheese mixture, sprinkling extra over the top. Shake off any extra breadcrumbs and with a great deal of care drop the eggs into some deep, very hot fat using a large perforated spoon. Allow them to cook for just a few moments, until they are golden brown. Remove and thoroughly drain. The parsley should be cooked in a separate batch of fat, again for a few moments. It should be crisp but remain perfectly green.

⇥ 130. EGGS IN BRIEF ⇤

Spain 1758. (Altamiras, 115)

Take pumpkin, onion, tomatoes, parsley and mint and fry, then place in a wide pot. Beat the eggs well, season with salt, place heat above and below until they set, then cut up like a tortilla and serve.

With its filling of pumpkin and tomatoes this makes an unusual and excellent *tortilla*, or Spanish omelet. In a modern Spanish kitchen, after the tortilla has been cooked thoroughly on one side it would be flipped over onto a saucepan lid and then turned over to cook on the other side. This recipe employs a different method. The tortilla is cooked in a pot placed over charcoal embers. However, to ensure the eggs are cooked thoroughly on top, additional hot coals are piled up on a lid placed over the tortilla.

⇥ 131. EGGS WITH HAZELNUT SAUCE ⇤

Spain 1758. (Altamiras, 115)

Take the hard-boiled eggs, shell and place in a pan of salted water. Fry lots of onion and add parsley, mint and also other spices and a sauce of hazelnuts, and set to simmer. Soak some bread in water and vinegar, then mince the nuts with two cloves of garlic. Add oil to the eggs with fried garlic, dilute the sauce with a little of the salted water. The sauce should be made to suit the number of eggs, and add the recado.

Garlic sauces made from ground hazelnuts are still popular in Spain. This very rustic dish is pungently flavored with its *recado*, or seasoning of parsley, mint, and garlic.

⇥ 132. FRITTATA WITH PROVATURA ⇤

Italy (Naples) 1790. (Leonardi, vol. 4, 156)

Beat twelve eggs with two provatura cheeses cut into small dice, a little grated parmesan, some salt, ground pepper, and a little bit of milk, or water. Melt a good piece of butter in a frying pan on a gentle fire; pour in the eggs; make the frittata in the usual way.

This frittata, a kind of thick omelet, is flavored with provatura, a buffalo milk cheese closely related to mozzarella. This mild rich cheese is sometimes smoked and this variant makes a delicious frittata. If you cannot get hold of genuine provatura, use mozzarella instead. The butter needs to be very hot before you pour in the egg mixture. Keep the eggs moving in the pan with a spatula. When the eggs are mostly cooked but still wet, you should stop stirring. There must be cooked egg scattered throughout, but loose egg in between. Let it stand on a low heat to ensure that the bottom of the frittata is well cooked. In the eighteenth century, a frittata was cooked entirely on top of a charcoal stove. It was sometimes carefully turned by flipping it onto a saucepan lid, a technique that takes practice and some nerve to get right. Nowadays it is more usual to cook the top of the frittata under a broiler or in the oven. Leonardi suggests that if the frittata gets stuck in the pan, a little water poured around it will loosen it and make it easier to remove in one piece. His contemporary Corrado gives us the excellent advice that a frittata should always be fried so the eggs are still tender and not overcooked. The recipe here is for a fairly simple frittata. Corrado gives some more unusual alternatives. One, made with fresh figs and Parmesan, is excellent. However, another with a filling made of dormice flesh would hardly be to modern taste!

SAUCES

⇥ 133. GENERAL PURPOSE COULIS ⇤

France 1755. (Les soupers de la cour, vol. 1, 72)

Garnish the bottom of a stew-pan with slices of ham, a little bacon fat and sufficient veal fillet; enough in quantity and goodness for making the coulis; put upon the meat two carrots, an onion stuck with cloves and a parsnip, and a small amount of meat stock; cook it on a slow fire, until the meat gives its juice, and then on a stronger fire, until it forms a fine brown caramel, i.e. a glaze round the stew-pan; put the pan on the fire again, with a good bit of butter worked with flour, and stir it continually with a spoon, until it is of a fine yellowish color; take proper care the fire is not so violent as to give it a burnt taste; then add as much stock and gravy as will keep it of a proper color and constituency; then put the meat back again, and simmer it a long while, skimming it often; when the meat is thoroughly done, take it out with a skimmer, and sift the coulis in a lawn sieve, or a sifting cloth, without pressing it.

This recipe explains how to make a very basic coulis. These highly savory meat concentrates were used both for adding flavor and for thickening sauces, soups, and stews. The meat removed from the coulis would have been used for another purpose.

⇥ 134. NUN'S SAUCE ⇤

France 1755. (Les soupers de la cour, vol. 1, 145)

Take slices of veal and ham, put them into a stewpan with a spoonful of oil, two or three mushrooms, a bouquet of parsley, green onions, a clove of garlic, two cloves, and half a leaf of laurel: let it catch on the fire, then add a glass of good broth, a little gravy, and a glass of Champagne: simmer it some time, skim it well (degrease), and rub through a sieve: when ready, add three or four green rocamboles, and a dozen of pistachio nuts whole.

This type of sauce is closely related to coulis, as it is a thick purée made by rubbing the meat and other ingredients through a sieve. A modern food processor will achieve the same result with far less effort. Rocamboles were a kind of green garlic. They were very popular in the eighteenth century; seeds are available from Heritage Seed companies, but spring onions or scallions make a good substitute.

⤳ 135. REMOULADE SAUCE ⤶

France 1755. (Les soupers de la cour, vol. 1, 143)

If you want it hot, slice two onions and fry them in oil; when they begin to color add a glass of white wine, as much bouillon, two slices of lemon, first peeled, two cloves of garlic, a laurel leaf, thyme, basil, and two cloves; boil a quarter of an hour, and rub through a sieve: add some chopped anchovy and capers, a spoonful of mustard, or horseradish reduced to a paste, pepper and salt: warm up without boiling.

This sauce is made cold, with chopped parsley, spring onions, shallots, a clove of garlic, anchovies and capers, a spoonful of mustard, or horseradish scraped very fine, a spoonful of oil, vinegar, course pepper and salt.

There were hot and cold versions of this pungent mustard or horseradish relish, which was one of the classic sauces of French haute cuisine. Instructions for both are offered here.

⤳ 136. RAVIGOTTE SAUCE ⤶

France 1755. (Les soupers de la cour, vol. 1, 134)

Chop a clove of garlic, chervil, burnet, tarragon, garden cresses, and chives, all in proportion to their flavor: when well washed and squeezed, infuse them in a little coulis without boiling: rub it through a sieve: then add a bit of butter, flour, pepper and salt: boil it to a good consistence, and add a lemon squeeze sufficient to make it relishing, or sharp-tasted.

Coulis was particularly important for adding substance and flavor to sauces that needed to be made rapidly. This herb and garlic sauce is related to the much older "green sauces" that had been popular since the medieval period.

ᛮ 137. BASIL SALSA ᛭

Italy (Kingdom of Naples) 1786. (Corrado, 187)

Melt in a pot a piece of butter seasoned with spices, and a quantity of minced basil, thicken this with egg yolks and lemon juice, and then serve the sauce on pigeons.

Pesto, made with basil, garlic, cheese, pine nuts, and olive oil, is one of the best-known Italian sauces. Commercially made versions are available in every supermarket. However, these manufactured varieties can never compete with a homemade pesto made with fresh basil. The sauce gets its name from the method used to incorporate the ingredients—pesto means bruised or trampled, as the sauce is ground with a pestle and mortar. Pesto hails from Liguria in northern Italy, but basil sauces were also made in other regions. Unlike pesto, this very simple basil salsa from eighteenth-century Naples was not designed to be eaten with pasta, but as an accompaniment to roast pigeon and other game birds.

ᛮ 138. RAISIN SALSA ᛭

Italy (Naples) 1786. (Corrado, 190)

Soften some raisins in muscatel wine, and grind with pine nuts, capers, and spices, dissolve it all in Malvasia wine, and season with some sugar and a bay leaf and let it boil, rub it through a sieve and serve over thrushes.

Although this rich raisin salsa was designed for serving with roasted thrushes, a bird we would not want to eat nowadays, it makes an attractive sauce for dressing quail or Cornish hen. The raisins need soaking overnight in sweet wine. If you cannot get Malvasia, use some Madeira or Marsala. Dissolve the raisin, caper, and pine nut paste in a little wine, add a bay leaf, and simmer the sauce gently to drive off the alcohol.

ᛮ 139. FLORENTINE SALSA ᛭

Italy (Naples) 1786. (Corrado, 190)

Grind a clove of garlic with some sage leaves, some raisins, candied citron, and a piece of fried liver, and the crumb of some bread soaked in rose vinegar, when this has all been dissolved together, boil it and season with sugar and spices; and then the sauce is served over liver.

Cooked liver was frequently used in Italian sauces, not only as a source of a rich flavor, but also as a means of achieving a smooth, silky texture. This rich garlic and sage salsa was designed to be served with fried calves' liver.

BREADS AND CAKES

◈ 140. TURIN BISCUIT OR SAVOY CAKE ◈

France 1755. (Les soupers de la cour, vol. 3, 284)

Take an equal weight of eggs and sugar; separate the yolks and whites; put the sugar to the yolks, with some lemon-peel finely chopped, powder of orange-flowers, or a spoonful of the water; beat up these very well together; and also the whites, which you mix with the yolks, stirring continuously, and half as much weight of flour as you used of eggs; pour it into the vessel you intend to bake it in, being first well rubbed with butter, and bake it in a soaking oven about an hour and an half.

These large molded sponges were very difficult to bake to perfection, and a well-formed Savoy cake was the mark of a highly skilled pastry cook. They were frequently cooked in very large ornamental copper molds, and cakes based on up to 60 eggs were not uncommon. To encourage an extra-large cake to rise properly, a special microclimate was often created in the oven by shoveling additional hot coals on to the baking tray on which the mold sat.[3] Cakes of this kind were notoriously difficult to remove from their molds. When butter was used to grease the mold, as in this recipe, it was usually clarified, though a mixture of clarified butter and calves' suet was preferred by some bakers. Sugar was usually sprinkled into the greased mold to create a hard candylike coating on the outside of the cake. If you have access to a large *kugelhopf* or *baba* mold it is well worth attempting one of these challenging cakes. The secret is to grease the mold with melted suet or clarified butter that is completely free of any water. Put a handful of caster sugar in the greased mold while it is still warm and move it around until it is evenly coated. Shake out the excess and pour the cake mixture in when the mold is completely cold. It should be filled to about three quarters full. It helps if a sheet of thick paper is tied round the mold as this retains the cake dough that rises above the top of the mold. The paper should protrude above the top of the mold by about three inches. When it is baked, you should leave it in the mold for about seven minutes before you attempt to tip it from the mold. The excess that rises above the mold should be trimmed off level with a bread knife.

◈ 141. TURK'S BONNET WITH ICE CREAM ◈

France 1755. (Les soupers de la cour, vol. 3, 284–285)

Make a clear paste, or batter as [in recipe 140]; and butter the mold, so called, in which it is to be baked; when it is cold, cut off the top gently, and a good deal of the inside; which dry in the oven, till it can be reduced to powder or crumbs. Boil a pint of cream and sugar according to judgment; reduce it to half, and add the crumbs to it: mix it well, to ice it to a certain degree, that you may

put it in the bonnet, and cover it over with the top to hide the cream: You may
masquerade the outside as you think proper, serve it plain, if of a good color.

A Savoy cake baked in a *kougelhopf* mold has a close resemblance to
a turban, thus the name Turk's Bonnet (sometimes Turk's Cap). This dish
is simply a hollowed-out Savoy cake filled with ice cream. However, the
excavated cake crumbs are added to the ice cream mix to produce a grainy-
textured biscuit ice cream, which was very popular in this period. In fact,
mixtures of this kind were sometimes frozen in molds to create fake ice
cream finger biscuits. In this recipe, the cream and sugar were gently simmered until they reduced to about half the volume. The biscuit crumbs were
then blended in before the mixture was frozen in a *sorbetière*. If you want to
make this dish, use three ounces of sugar to a pint of cream. To masquerade,
or mask, a dish was to decorate it in some way. This kind of cake was often
covered in sugar icing and ornamented.

SWEET PASTRIES AND PUDDINGS

⊰ 142. TO MAKE A TRIFLE ⊱

England 1751. (Glasse, 284)

Cover the bottom of your dish or bowl with Naples biscuits broke in pieces,
macaroons broke in halves, and ratafia cakes. Just wet them all through with
sack, then make a good boiled custard not too thick, and when cold pour it
over it, then put a syllabub over that. You may garnish it with ratafia cakes,
currant jelly and flowers.

At the time of Shakespeare, a trifle was a simple thickened cream flavored with rosewater or spice. By the middle of the eighteenth century it
had become a layered dish, usually made by soaking biscuit or cake in wine
and custard and topping them with a creamy alcoholic whip called a syllabub. This was frequently decorated with colorful sugar comfits, tiny ratafia biscuits, or even fresh or candied flowers. Naples biscuit was a generic
name for dried sponge biscuit. Ratafias were bitter almond-flavored cookies
almost identical to Italian *amaretti*. This is the earliest printed English recipe for a layered trifle. It appeared in the fourth edition of Hannah Glasse's
The Art of Cookery Made Plain and Easy (London, 1751). To make the syllabub, see recipe 146.

⊰ 143. APPLE FRITTERS ON PEDESTALS ⊱

France 1755. (Les soupers de la cour, vol. 4, 16)

Cut twelve good baking apples in two; leave them whole if small ones; peel
them, and take out the pips with a corer; marinate them three or four hours in

brandy, sugar, orange-flower water, and lemon-peel; drain and flour them to fry in a very hot boiling fat, and glaze them with sugar and a hot salamander or shovel. The pedestals are made with bits of puff-paste baked, cut with puits-d'amour molds; raise them properly upon each other, arranged as you think proper.

These delicious apple fritters, covered in a glaze of caramelized sugar, sit attractively on little pedestals of puff pastry. To make the marinade, finely grate some lemon zest into a bowl, and add two tablespoons of sugar, a cup of brandy, and a tablespoon of orange flower water. When the prepared apples have soaked in this mixture for about four hours, drain them and roll them in plain white flour. Deep-fry them for a few minutes until the apples are soft and the coating of flour turns golden brown. Dust them with powdered sugar and glaze them with a hot salamander or blowtorch. A *puits d'amour* mold was a tin cutter that enabled a ring shape to be stamped out of pastry. *Puits d'amour* were puff pastry rings filled with fruit preserves that were thought to resemble wells, thus the name, which means "wells of love." Use two circular tin pastry cutters to achieve the same result. The larger should be about the same diameter as your apple pieces. Cut your rings from puff pastry rolled out to about a quarter of an inch thickness. Brush them with a little beaten egg yolk and bake them in a hot oven until they have risen and cooked to a golden brown. Do not bake them in a convection oven as this will cause them to rise at an angle.

⊰ 144. AN APRICOT CUSTARD ⊱

England 1758. (Moxon, 134)

Take a pint of cream, boil it with a stick of cinnamon and six eggs (leave out four of the whites) when your cream is a little cold, mix your eggs and cream together, with a quarter of a pound of fine sugar, set it over a slow fire, stir it all one way whilst it is begin to be thick, then take it off and stir it whilst it be a little cold, and pour it into your dish; take six apricots, as you did for your pudding, rather a little higher; when they are cold lie them upon your custard at equal distances; if it be at the time that you have no ripe apricots, you may lie preserved apricots.

Georgian England was celebrated for its wide variety of cream dishes and custards. This is one of the best. However, the instructions for the custard are a little confusing for a modern cook. It is important to understand that the author intends the reader to first gently boil the cinnamon in the cream without the eggs. A good tip to prevent the cream sticking to the pan is to mix the sugar in at this stage. Allow the cream to cool before adding the beaten egg and then gently cook while continuously stirring to make the custard. For a really luxurious result make the custard with heavy cream.

The author refers here to a previous recipe for an apricot pudding in which she explains how to cook the apricots. Cut six apricots in half, core them, put them in a saucepan with three ounces of sugar, and gently cook them until the sugar dissolves. Continue to cook them until they turn transparent, but do not allow them to disintegrate into jam. Allow them to cool and arrange on top of your cold custard.

⇥ 145. A TART DE MAY ⇤

England 1760. (Bradley, vol. 1, 257)

Provide a good quantity of sweet meats and some fine marrow, make a puff paste crust, lat it round the dish, and then begin to lay in the ingredients: First put in a layer of biscuit to cover the bottom of the dish, then put over this a layer of marrow, with some butter among it, upon this put a layer of various sweetmeats, the more sorts the better; over this put more biscuits, then marrow, and so on till the dish is full. When this is done set on a quart of cream, let it boil, thicken it with four eggs, and pour in one spoonful of orange-flower water, then add some treble refined loaf sugar, beaten to powder, till it is sweetened to the palate; pour this upon the ingredients in the dish, and send it to the oven. Half an hour will bake it very well.

This rich citrus peel and custard tart was very popular in England in the eighteenth century, though in most other recipe books it is normally called a *tart du moy*. Both *may* and *moy* are corrupt English versions of the French word *moëlle*, meaning bone marrow. This rich fat, found in the center of large beef and veal bones, was once a popular ingredient in many sweet puddings, adding an unctuous richness that was much admired. Once removed from the bones it was left to soak in water for a few hours to remove traces of blood and bone fragments. If you cannot get hold of bone marrow, just add a little more butter to achieve a similar effect. Tarts of this kind were usually baked in a pastry case, but in this version the ingredients are placed in an unlined pie plate. However, a ring of puff pastry is arranged round the rim of the dish, which when it rises, acts as a kind of pastry reservoir surrounding the filling. To achieve this you need to make your tart in a metal plate rather than a pan. Arrange your puff pastry ring on the rim of the plate. By biscuit is meant sponge—trifle sponges or sponge fingers are ideal. Sweetmeats were preserved citrus peels—orange, lemon, and citron were the favorites.

⇥ 146. EVERLASTING WHIP SYLLABUB
TO PUT INTO GLASSES ⇤

England 1789. (Nutt, 98)

TAKE five half pints of thick cream, half a pint of Rhenish wine, half a pint of sack, and the juice of two large Seville oranges; rasp in the yellow rind of three lemons, and a pound of double refined sugar well pounded and sifted; mix all together with a spoonful of orange-flower water, beat it well together with a whisk half an hour, then, with a spoon fill your glasses. This will keep above a week; it is much better for being made the day before it is used.

Syllabubs were very light frothy alcoholic creams. They had been popular in England since the sixteenth century and were usually served in specialized glasses. They were also used as toppings for centerpiece dishes like the trifle above. This recipe makes a very large quantity of syllabub. At this time an English pint was equivalent to 16 fluid ounces, and this must be understood if you intend to reduce the quantities in order to make a more modest amount. The technique requires beating all of the ingredients in a large bowl with a good sized balloon whisk until it starts to become like whipped cream. Spoon it into jelly or wine glasses. Or use the recipe to make the syllabub topping for the trifle in recipe 142.

CONFECTIONS

❊ 147. DIABLOTINS OR LITTLE DEVILS ❊

France 1755. (Les soupers de la cour, vol. 4, 336)

This is done with chocolate pounded, made malleable with some good oil, and formed into a hard paste; roll bits of it in the hand in the form of nuts, olives, or pistachios, or any other shapes, either round or flat; stick bits of sugared cinnamon here and there, and strew them with nonpareils of different colors; you may also put a nut in each of the different kinds of fruits you propose to imitate; dry these in the same manner as all sugared fruits.

This is one of the earliest recipes for making chocolates. There are earlier confections made using chocolate, like the biscuits in recipe 95, but *diablotins* are really the precursors of our modern chocolate sweets. Chocolate at this period was made on a *metate* and was much higher in cocoa solids than modern chocolate. This allowed it to be softened in a warm mortar or in the hands without melting. Mexican metate, ground chocolate, can sometimes be found in specialist ships. If you can get hold of some, try rolling a piece of it the size of an almond in between your hands until it softens and turns into a ball. Anoint your hands first in a little almond oil. Once it has formed, drop it in a dish full of small colored comfits or sprinkles. Nonpareils were small colored comfits. This sugary coating enabled the diablotins to be picked up without melting in the fingers.

❊ 148. NAPLES BISCUIT ❊

England 1789. (Nutt, 5)

Take one pound and a half of Lisbon sugar, put it into a little copper saucepan, and three quarters of a pint (wine measure) of water in with the sugar, and one small cup full of orange flower water, and boil the sugar with the water till it is all melted; then break twelve eggs, whites and yolks together, whisk them well, then pour the Lisbon syrup boiling hot in with the eggs, and whisk them as fast as you can at the time of pouring in the syrup, or the eggs will spoil; when you have poured it all in, keep whisking it till it is quite cold and set; when it is cold, take one pound and a half of flour, and mix it as light as possible; then put two sheets of paper on the copper plate you bake on, and take one sheet of paper and make the edges of it stand up about an inch and a half high, and pour your batter in it, sift some powdered sugar over it, and put it in the oven; attend it carefully, to prevent its burning on the top; do not leave the oven one minute, when you think it is near baked enough; and when baked, take it out in the paper, and let it stand till cold, then turn it over, and wet the bottom of the paper till the paper comes off with ease; then cut it to what size you like: you may bake it in small tins, if more convenient.

This type of dried sponge biscuit was made in Naples, where it was called *pan de spagna*. It was usually made by baking sponge biscuit batter in paper cases. In England, where it was commonly known as Naples biscuit, it was an important stock ingredient in many pudding and sweet recipes. After baking it was usually cut into slices and put back into a cool oven to dehydrate. Nutt may have learned this recipe from his master, the Turin confectioner Domenico Negri. It is the only accurate recipe for making Naples biscuit in any English cookbook. Lisbon sugar was a partially refined sugar and was probably rather like a modern pale brown sugar. A wine-measure pint was equivalent to 16 fluid ounces.

Houléte

Sarbotiere

Sarbotiere et son Seau

Ice cream–making equipment of the eighteenth century. The pewter freezing pot or sorbetière *sits in a wooden pail of ice and salt. When the mixture starts to freeze, it is scrapped down with the spaddle or* houléte.

ICES

⊰ 149. RED CURRANT WATER ICE ⊱

France 1751. (Menon, La science du maître d'hôtel cuisinier, *51)*

Take two pounds of redcurrants, and the quantity of a pound of raspberries; put them all in a pot, cook them for three or four "covered boilings," you then push them through a sieve in order to get the juice, which you will simmer over the stove, next you take a pound and a half of sugar, which you dissolve over the fire in the juice, add a chopine of water, and then put it in a ceramic pot in order to cool it down, next you place your redcurrant water in a freezing pot in order to make a water ice.

The blend of red currants and raspberries in this water ice makes an exquisitely flavored water ice of intense color. A *chopine* was more or less equivalent to a modern pint. Freeze the mixture in a churn ice cream maker.

ᕴ 150. ARTICHOKE NEIGE ᕬ

France 1751. (Gilliers, 158)

Take three or four artichokes, from which you will only use the bottoms; blanch them until they are quite soft; crush them with four ounces of cleansed pistachios, and a piece of preserved orange peel, and a little cream; pass this paste through a sieve; mix this with a pint of cream, cooked in the same manner... add to this some powder sugar according to your taste; pass all of this through a sieve and put it in a freezing pot.

In France, ices were normally called *glaces*, but for a brief period in the middle of the eighteenth century some varieties were given the alternative name of *neige*, meaning snow. This one is unusual, as it is flavored with globe artichoke bottoms. In an earlier recipe Gilliers has already explained how to make a basic cream *neige*, in which he uses three egg yolks to a pint of cream. So, to make this recipe, beat up three egg yolks and four ounces of sugar in a pint of cream and warm it gently in a saucepan. Continuously stir with a wooden spoon until it forms custard, but do not allow it to boil—the custard is ready when it starts to coat the spoon. Remove the skins from the pistachios by pouring boiling water over them. Leave them to soak for about half an hour, and then rub them briskly between the palms of your hands and pick out the skins. Pound them in a mortar. When the custard has cooled add the puree of artichokes, the minced preserved orange, and the pounded pistachios. Freeze in an ice cream maker.

ᕴ 151. WATERMELON SORBETTO ᕬ

Italy (Naples) 1778. (Corrado, 12)

Pass the flesh of a very mature watermelon through a sieve, and blend it with a carafe of very dense syrup, season with cinnamon water and put it in the freezing pot to coagulate.

Make the syrup from the instructions given after recipe 152. A Neapolitan carafe was equivalent to about a pint and a half. This quantity would be about right for a very large watermelon or two smaller ones. If you want to be more scientific, use a quarter pint of the stock syrup to every pint of watermelon pulp. See recipe 94 for instructions for making cinnamon water.

✦ NEAPOLITAN SORBET AND ICE CREAM FLAVORS 1778

Citron	Candied Egg	Raspberry	Pink Cinnamon
Cherry	Chocolate	Violet	Imperial
Portugal Orange	Torron	Watermelon	Pistachio
Muscat Pear	Milk	Fresh Fennel	White Cinnamon
Chestnut	Muscatel Grape	Melon	Lime
English Milk	Peach	Mixed Fruit	Pistachio Milk
Pomegranate	Pineapple	Orgeat	Jasmine
Butter	Venetian	Sour Milk	Chocolate Spuma
Milk Spuma[4]			

❧ 152. PARMESAN CHEESE ICE CREAM ❧

England 1789. (Nutt, 125)

Take six eggs, half a pint of syrup and a pint of cream put them into a stewpan and boil them until it begins to thicken; then rasp three ounces of parmesan cheese, mix and pass them through a sieve, and freeze it.

Though it sounds outlandish, this is a remarkable ice cream. It is very creamy and has a subtle taste of cheese. It is what the French called a *fromage glace*—frozen cheese. Nutt's recipe is derived from an earlier French version in which the ice was molded into a wedge of cheese and given a fake rind made out of caramelized sugar. In all of Nutt's ice cream recipes we are directed to use what confectioners called stock syrup—see the next recipe. Use it also for making the two following recipes, which are also from Nutt's book.

✦ TO MAKE STOCK SYRUP

1000 mls of water and 1 kg of sugar

Bring the water to the boil and remove from the heat. Add the sugar and stir until dissolved. When cool store in a large jar and keep it in a cold place until required.

❧ 153. ROYAL ICE CREAM ❧

England 1789. (Nutt, 118)

Take the yolks of ten eggs and two whole eggs; beat them up well with your spoon; then take the rind of one lemon, two gills of syrup, one pint of cream, a little spice, and a little orange flower water; mix them all well and put them over the fire, stirring them all the time with your spoon; when you find it grows thick take it off, and pass it through a sieve; put it into a freezing pot, freeze it, and take a little citron, and lemon and orange peel with a few pistachio nuts blanched; cut them all and mince them with your ice before you put them in your molds.

A mold for making a wedge of Parmesan ice cream.

At this period ices were frequently molded into the forms of fruits, vegetables, animals, birds, and other novelty items. A gill was a quarter of a pint.

❧ 154. BURNT FILBERT ICE CREAM ❧

England 1789. (Nutt, 123)

Roast some Barcelona nuts well in the oven, and pound them a little with some cream; put four eggs into a stew pan, with one pint of cream and two gills of syrup; boil it till it grows thick, pass it through a sieve and freeze it; then mix your filberts with it before you put it in your molds.

Barcelona nuts were high quality filberts or hazelnuts imported into England from Spain. Use standard hazelnuts. A gill was a quarter of a pint.

4

🕊 THE REIGN OF NAPOLEON TO THE VICTORIAN ERA, 1800–1850

Although the French lost the Napoleonic Wars (1792–1815), the triumphant progress of their culinary art was much more successful in conquering the taste buds of nineteenth-century Europe. Despite the chaos of war and all its privations, dining on a grand scale continued unabated at countless victory banquets and celebration balls. Paris remained an important destination on the grand tour, and its newly established restaurants, dining clubs, and cafes were serving food of a quality that could only have been experienced in wealthy private households before the Revolution. One of the most important restaurateurs in the city was Antoine Beauvilliers, the former chef to King Louis XVI's brother and the founder of La Grande Taverne de Londres in 1782. He based the idea for his establishment on the London Tavern, a very grand eating house in London's Bishopsgate. Beauvilliers's cookbook, *l'Art du cuisinier* (1814), affords an interesting insight into the variety of dishes that were served in an early Parisian restaurant.

One of Beauvilliers's rivals, the pastry cook Antonin Carême, was the most influential figure in the culinary world at this time. A temperamental, artistic genius, Carême was abandoned as a child by his poverty-stricken father outside a Paris pastry shop. The kindly proprietor brought the child up and engaged him as an apprentice. Despite this unpromising beginning, Carême eventually went on to work for the Prince de Tallyrand, the Prince Regent of England, Czar Alexander of Russia, and the Rothschild family. A prolific author, his numerous books were illustrated with line drawings of his remarkable culinary creations. Like the confectioners of the *ancien regime*,

A suckling pig galantine. This design by An-tonin Carême shows an entrée dish deco-rated with silver skewers called hatelets. *Each* hatelet *is garnished with two black truffles that sandwich a small molded gela-tin. The stand is made of an inedible pastry called* pâte d'office.

Carême created fairy-tale tabletop scenes of pagodas, Classical ruins, and Turkish minarets. However, he also extended his artistic imagination to the savory dishes of the meal, which were often as decorative as his *pièces montées* (pastry centerpieces). Carême's culinary style shaped upper-class food for the rest of the century.

Enthusiasm for French cooking among the English aristocracy reached an all-time high in this period and a number of émi-gré chefs established themselves as culi-nary celebrities in Britain. Among these was Eustace Ude, who had worked in the household of Louis XVI and became cook to the Earl of Sefton. In the introduction to *The French Cook* (1813), he lamented British attitudes toward the status of the culinary professional: "In England, the few assistants that a head cook is allowed in a family, and the number of dishes he has to prepare, often deprive him of an opportunity of dis-playing his abilities; nay, after ten years of the utmost exertion to bring his Art to per-fection, he ranks no higher than an humble domestic."[1]

The other notable French chef of this period, who went on to become a household name in Victorian England, was Alexis Soyer. An eccentric show-man and entrepreneur, his most important book was *The Gastronomic Regen-erator* (1846), a treatise on high-class cooking, though he also penned other works aimed at lower social groups. Soyer's rival, Charles Elmé Francatelli, a protégé of Carême, worked for a brief time for Queen Victoria but left her service because he was dissatisfied with the kitchens at Buckingham Palace, which from time to time flooded with sewage! He tended to be over-shadowed by Soyer, but Francatelli's masterwork, *The Modern Cook* (1846), affords a much better glimpse into the nature of Anglo-French fine cooking at this time than the verbose books of his flamboyant contemporary.

Despite the domination of French haute cuisine on upper-class tables and in the culinary literature, the first half of the nineteenth century saw a resurging interest in national and regional cookery traditions. In the Italian peninsula, Antonio Nebbia's *Il cuoco Milanase* (1829) extolled the virtues of the regional cuisine of Lombardy, though it does contain a lot of French-derived recipes. A similar phenomenon occurred in German-speaking parts of Europe. The anonymous *Die sich selbst lehrende köchin* (1803) gives recipes for dishes from the city of Hamburg. There are directions for making archetypal baked goods from the Germanic folk tradition like *stollen* (German Christmas cake) and *lebkuchenherz* (gingerbread hearts), though the latter is rather unusually flavored with cardamom (see recipe 191). Published in Cologne in 1846, *Kleine kölner köchin* includes a range of suet puddings, one of them made from the local black rye bread. These little books were targeted at quite ordinary households. By the middle of the century, mechanized printing methods led to many cheap cookbooks targeted at literate, working-class housewives.

Soups

⊰ 155. GREEN PEA SOUP ⊱

France 1814. (Beauvilliers, vol. 1, 21)

Take a sufficient quantity of peas, put them into a pot with onions, carrots, a bunch of leeks, and celery, with a bone, or some slices of ham or bacon; if they are old, let them be steeped the night before; if new, use them immediately; toss them in butter, with a handful of parsley and small onions; wet them with good stock; when they are soaked enough, drain, and beat them in a mortar, put them through a sieve, with the juice that was drained out of them; put it into a saucepan, and let it simmer four or five hours; stir it often, that it may not stick; skim before stirring it; when it is done, serve it over rice, vermicelli, or fried bread, which must be added at the moment of serving.

At most European high-class nineteenth-century dinners there were usually two types of soup on offer—a thick soup, or *purée*, and a clear soup, or *consommé*. Thick soups based on peas and fortified with ham have been popular throughout Europe since the medieval period and were enjoyed by all classes. This hearty purée retains some medieval characteristics, like the manner of serving it over pieces of fried bread.

✦ SOUPS ON THE MENU AT BEAUVILLIERS'S RESTAURANT AT 142 PALAIS ROYAL, PARIS, C. 1800

Lettuce soup	Puree soup with croutons	Cabbage soup
Consommé	Printannier soup	Puree soup
Almond milk soup	Crayfish bisque	Turtle soup
Bread soup	Soup of health	Vermicelli soup
Rice soup	Julienne soup	

⇥ 156. CLEAR SORREL SOUP ⇤

France 1833. (Carême, vol. 1, 265)

Cut and wash a large handful of sorrel, a lettuce, and some chervil, sauté them with some bacon scraped, melted, and strained through a sieve, or else use fresh butter; then put it to the consommé, prepared as usual, add a pinch of sugar, and skim the soup, boil it an hour and a half, and pour it into the tureen, with croutons prepared as usual: the sorrel passed with bacon is the most savory.

Most of Carême's soups are complex preparations. This one, however, is a simple sorrel soup that is easy to prepare if you have some ready-made consommé to hand (see recipe 158). Scraped bacon is minced bacon fat.

⇥ 157. PROFITEROLE SOUP À LA WAGRAM ⇤

France 1833. (Carême, vol. 1, 177)

The day before serving the soup, order at the baker's fifteen small round rolls (called profiteroles), two inches in diameter; they should have a fine color, and not be rasped; three-quarters of an hour before serving, open them at the top like the petits choux when to be filled with cream, and having taken out all the crumb, fill them with a quenelle of fowl with crayfish butter worked with it, re-cover them with the crust cut out, but preserved for this purpose; soak these crusts in some reduced consommé for some seconds, then drain and arrange them on a buttered saute-pan over some hot ashes that the quenelle may have time allowed to be done enough without the rolls taking color or catching; cover them, and put fire over them also; when they are done, which may be known by uncovering the small hole, and if the quenelle be firm, place them carefully in the tureen, adding the tails of fifty crayfish, the shells of which were used in making the butter for the quenelles; add fifty button mushrooms passed and drained, some blanched chervil, and the points of a bundle of large asparagus carefully blanched; when serving, pour upon them consommé prepared as usual with a little sugar and grated nutmeg.

This elaborate soup illustrates perfectly the French modular system of cookery. All of the stock ingredients required to make it would have been at hand in a sizeable kitchen at this period. Quenelle pastes of various flavors were always at the chef's disposal (see recipe 163). These delicate preparations were made by combining pounded meat or fish with a bread- or flour-based thickening agent called panada. A range of clarified consommés, too, were kept hot and ready for use in large copper pots (see recipe 158). Crayfish butter was a good way of recycling the shells of this tasty crustacean; an assistant would ensure that this was carefully prepared and ready for use (see recipe 171). It was probably also the same assistant's job to hollow the profiteroles and fill them with the quenelle mixture. Profiteroles at this period were small hollowed-out bread rolls—they gave their name to the familiar sweet choux pastries filled with cream. The soup was named in honor of the Battle of Wagram (July 5–6, 1809), which was Napoleon's last victorious battle.

⊰ 158. CONSOMMÉ OF FOWLS FOR SOUPS ⊱

England 1846. (Francatelli, 214)

Take two or more fowls, according to the quantity of broth required; roast them before a brisk fire until half done; and then put them into a small well-tinned stockpot, nearly filled up with water, and place this on the fire to boil; skim the consommé, and then add one good-sized carrot, two turnips, one onion, one head of celery, two cloves, a small piece of mace, and a little salt. Set the stock on the side of the stove to boil gently for about two hours, and then strain it off for use. This kind of consommé is admirably adapted for persons of delicate health as a restorative. It is also very serviceable in imparting delicacy of flavor to all clear soups.

A consommé is a stock that has been clarified. This was achieved by adding whipped egg whites, allowing it to boil, and then straining it through a cloth jelly bag. Crushed eggshells were sometimes also added to the stock. Like the egg whites, these helped the liquid to separate out from any residue. The cooked egg whites also blocked the mesh of the jelly bag, making it even more efficient. If you want to try it, make the stock described as in the recipe. First of all strain it through a colander to remove any vegetables or pieces of chicken. Put the stock back in the saucepan and let it simmer. Whip up two or three egg whites and incorporate them into the cooking stock with a balloon whisk. The egg whites will start to rise up to the top of the saucepan. Remove from the heat before it boils over and let the egg whites fall. Repeat this process three times and then strain through a jelly bag.

⊰ 159. PALESTINE SOUP ⊱

England 1846. (Francatelli, 73)

Cleanse, peel, wash, and slice up half a peck of Jerusalem artichokes; put them into a stew pan with four ounces of fresh butter, and allow them to simmer gently on a slow fire, until they are reduced in quantity and partially melted—taking care that they do not get colored in the process. Then add two quarts of strong white consommé of fowl, and after allowing it to boil gently for three quarters of an hour, proceed to rub the whole through a tammy-cloth in the usual way, and clarify the purée. Just before sending to table, add a pint of boiling cream, a small piece of glaze, and a little pounded sugar.

Francatelli may have learned how to make this soup when he worked under Carême, who was its inventor. By glaze, Francatelli meant a meat concentrate called meat glaze, which was added as a flavor enhancer. It was made by reducing a stock or gravy by careful simmering until it turned into a thick glue-like jelly. It was melted and painted on to cooked meats to enhance the surface with an attractive glossy varnish. A tammy-cloth was a linen cloth used as a strainer.

MEAT

⊰ 160. BOAR'S HEAD IN GALANTINE ⊱

France 1828. (Carême, 139–143)

Cut the head from the boar as close to the shoulders as possible, so as that all the neck should be with it, the only method of obtaining the head in its beauty; singe it carefully, above all burn the ears, scrape it perfectly, and bone it, by cutting it lengthwise underneath; be careful not to cut the skin with the knife; this operation finished, lay the head in a large glazed pan, and rub it with four ounces of seasoning spice, and one ounce of saltpeter, very finely pounded, and strew over it bay-leaves, thyme, basil, grated nutmeg, cloves, and a few juniper berries, two carrots, two large onions sliced, and whole parsley; two days after rub it again with this seasoning, and leave it from four to six days in this state; then lift it on a large dish, and carefully pick off all the herbs and roots, and wipe it with a napkin; cut away some of the meat from the thick part of the neck, and lay those pieces on the muzzle part, to render it more equal in thickness; then cover the surface half an inch thick, with a forcemeat thus prepared: chop one pound of fresh pork with one pound and a half of fat bacon, add seasoning spice, pound and mix with it four eggs, some sweet herbs chopped and passed in butter, with half a pound of the lean of a Bayonne ham chopped fine, and some truffles chopped also; then prepare large lardoons of bacon of an unequal size, two tongues salted red, two udders dressed in consommé, four pounds of truffles, and half a pound of pistachio kernels; lay on the farce a layer of truffle, tongue, udder, and pistachios, and cover them with a little farce: prepare also a fine fleshy turkey as a galantine, and lay it within the head, add the remaining farce, lardoons, &c. as above named, with a little seasoning with the lardoons; give the head its original shape, and sew the two sides together, cover the head entirely with bards of bacon, lay it on a large napkin, in which tie it up as tight as possible, and observe that the ears are kept in their natural position, then sew the napkin to preserve the form of the head: lay in a large brazing kettle the skins of the bacon you have used, lay the head upon them, with two knuckles of veal, the carcass of the turkey, two large bundles of sweet herbs, six carrots, and six onions stuck with six cloves each; pour into the kettle one or two bottles of Madeira wine, half a pint of brandy, and stock to cover the head entirely, with the skimming from a consommé of fowl, and a buttered paper; let it boil slowly over a bed of cinders, with fire on the top also, for five hours; try it with the point of a skewer, and if it quits easily it is done enough, but if difficultly let it boil for another hour; leave it to cool in its braize; then drain it carefully on a large dish, and when quite cold take off the cloth and the bacon, wipe it with a napkin, and rub it with a little oil, then having perfectly wiped it, glaze it with a glaze of a deep red color, and fix the tusks in their proper place. The decoration is formed with branches of yew and roses of wax, which are placed in a wreath on the top of the head (see the design); the two laurel wreaths surrounding the escutcheon should be cut from leaves of the almond laurel; the escutcheon is cut from a sheet of wax one-sixth of an inch thick; for this purpose spread on a stew pan cover some wax, which harden on ice, ornament this shield with stripes of rose-colored pâte d'office; as for the eyes, cut them of the natural size with the point of a knife, take off their skin, and fill the vacancy with wax, imitating the pupil with a round piece of truffle; if you place two small rose-colored wax in the glandules, or small marks found on each side of the nose, and shade this rose with white, the eye becomes as if animated, and the head has a fine effect; place a cypher or initials on the shield: thus decorated, fix it on a socle, or on a dish with a napkin. The turkey may be omitted without altering the quality of the galantine, but it will not be so well colored in the cutting; a fowl must therefore be used in its stead. The other head is the same, with a different decoration only.

With its stuffing of Bayonne ham, a whole boned turkey, tongues, and a staggering five pounds of black truffles, this recipe is included here to illustrate the extravagance and technical virtuosity of Carême's culinary art. He has frequently been accused of writing overly long, complex recipes. However, his intention was to describe every process required in the greatest possible detail. A decorated wild boar's head had been a centerpiece dish since the early medieval period, usually for Christmas entertainments. However, there are no surviving recipes from the middle ages and it seems that Carême's ambitious instructions were the first to be published. It was a difficult dish to prepare, requiring advanced butchery skills to remove the skull from the head without spoiling its appearance. Plenty of time also had to be allowed for the lengthy pickling process. Once the head had been filled with the farce, it was sewn up and tightly bound in a cloth. This was to prevent it from losing its shape in the five-hour boiling process. A boiled meat preparation of this kind supported by a wrapping of cloth was called a *galantine,* thus the name of the dish. The turkey galantine used in the stuffing was made in the same way. *Pâte d'office* was a fine inedible pastry that was used solely for decorative purposes. A socle was an ornamental stand, often sculpted from lard or molded in wax.

Designs for galantine of boar's head.

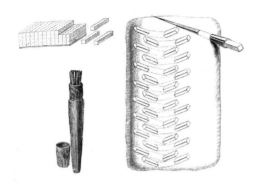

Larding pins and techniques.

☙ 161. ITALIAN BEEF ❧

Italy (Lombardy) 1829. (Luraschi, 53)

Spike a piece of beef with lardoons and garlic, make ready a little bed of butter, some fat, onions, celery, carrots and slices of bacon, and above this bed place the beef, make it brown, turn it round a number of times, and after it has browned pour over a half pint of white wine, allow it to boil until dry, put in some good stock, cover well, leaving it all to cook for five or more hours on a slow fire, degrease, and serve with its cooking sauce passed through a sieve, and if you please you can serve it with a garniture of little onions.

This simple, everyday beef stew is made by first preparing what a modern Italian cook would call a *sofritto*. Luraschi refers to this as the "bed" of butter, vegetables, and bacon fried under the meat. The recipe is from northern Italy, so butter and bacon fat are used instead of olive oil. If you want to replicate this dish, cut some deep holes into a good sized piece of topside and push some garlic cloves into them. Cut some lardoons of bacon fat and sew them into the meat with a larding pin. Follow Luraschi's instructions, browning the meat well and turning it every now and then. Pour in the wine and allow it to bubble fiercely until it reduces down to a thick glaze at the bottom of the pan. Then cover the meat with the stock. It was probably originally cooked with coals both below and above, a technique the French called *à la braize*. Luraschi takes it for granted that the cook will know exactly how much seasoning to add. Toward the end of the long cooking process, poach 20 to 30 baby onions in stock and use them to garnish the beef. Rub all of the cooked vegetables and stock through a sieve and pour it over the joint for sauce.

POULTRY AND GAME

☙ 162. CHARTREUSE OF VEGETABLES, GARNISHED WITH PARTRIDGES ❧

England 1846. (Francatelli, 239)

Scrape eight large carrots, and parboil them in water with a little salt for ten minutes; then put them to boil in some broth with a little sugar and salt, and a small pat of butter; when done, place them on a dish in the larder to get cold. In the mean time, eight large turnips should be peeled, and boiled in the same way as the carrots, and then put on a dish to cool. Next, a plain round mould must be lined with buttered paper, and the prepared carrots and turnips cut into appropriate forms or shapes for the purpose of arranging them over the bottom and round the inside of the mould, taking care that they fit in with each other, so as to represent any of the foregoing designs. Meanwhile parboil three large Savoy cabbages in water; then immerse them in cold water, after which squeeze the moisture from them; spread them upon a napkin on the table, take out the cores, season with mignonette-pepper and salt, and tie each up with string. Then, put the cabbages into a large stew pan with three partridges trussed with their legs inside, one pound of streaky bacon (previously parboiled), and two large saveloys; season with two onions stuck with four cloves, two carrots, and a garnished faggot; moisten with three pints of stock, cover with a buttered paper, put on the lid, and set them to braize gently for about two hours, if the birds are young, or three hours if not. When done, drain the cabbage into a colander, put the partridges, bacon, and saveloys on a dish to cool; squeeze broth from the cabbage by pressing it tightly in a strong kitchen rubber; then chop it and afterwards put it into a stew pan with a spoonful of brown sauce, and stir it quickly over a brisk fire until it resembles a somewhat firm paste. Use this preparation to garnish the bottom and sides of the chartreuse, about an inch thick. The partridges must be cut up neatly into small members, tossed in enough brown sauce to moisten them, and then placed in the cavity of chartreuse in close order, so as to give it solidity when turned out of the mould on its dish; a layer of prepared cabbage should be put over these, and the whole covered with a circular piece of buttered paper. An hour before dinner, the chartreuse must be placed in a stew pan with sufficient water to reach up only one-third the height the mould; then set the lid on, and put the stew pan near or upon a slow fire to keep the water gently simmering, so that the steam warms the chartreuse through. When about to serve, turn the chartreuse up-side-down in the dish, and draw the mould off with care, remove the paper, and garnish the base with a close border of the bacon and saveloys cut into scollops; pour some brown sauce (worked with essence of vegetables) round the entree, glaze the chartreuse carefully, so as not to disturb the order of the vegetables, and serve.

These directions will serve for the preparation of several kinds of chartreuses: pheasant, duckling, pigeons, &c., being substituted for partridges.

These decorative entrée dishes were a specialty of Carême and his talented pupil Francatelli. They are technically demanding but well worth the trouble. This recipe is for a very large chartreuse, so if you want to attempt it, you will need to divide Francatelli's quantities by three. You will require a charlotte mold or deep round cake tin. Cut a circle of well-oiled greaseproof paper that will fit in the base and carefully line the sides with a long strip of greaseproof paper. Use the fattest carrots you can find. Cut slices from the carrots and the turnips about an eighth of an inch thick. If you do not have any small oblong pastry cutters, make a thick cardboard template and cut your shapes from the slices with a sharp knife. They should all be

Illustrations for vegetable chartreuses.

identical in size. Since this is your first attempt, try a simple checkerboard pattern of alternating carrot and turnip before you have a go at any more complex designs. Make the base first and then build up the sides a row at a time, sticking your vegetable slices on to the sides of the lined mold with some cold butter. A saveloy is a type of smoked sausage. Mignonette pepper is a mixture of coarsely ground black and white pepper. If you have some meat glaze use that instead of brown sauce. Remove the chartreuse from the mold with a great deal of care.

⊰ 163. QUENELLE OF FOWL ⊱

England 1846. (Francatelli, 58)

Take of panada and prepared udder, or fresh butter, half a pound of each, to these add ten ounces of prepared fillets of chicken, as directed above, and pound all three together in a mortar; when they are well mixed, add salt, and as much grated nutmeg as will cover a sixpence, a little pepper, and one egg; pound the whole together till thoroughly mixed, then add another whole egg and two yolks, and a tablespoonful of Béchamel or Supreme sauce. Pound the whole thoroughly and quickly, and after having taken the force-meat out of the mortar and put it into a kitchen basin, keep it in a cool place until wanted for use.

Previously to taking the quenelle up out of the mortar, its consistency should be thus ascertained. Take a piece of the force-meat the size of a large nut, roll it with a little flour into the form of a round ball, put it into a small stewpan half full of boiling water; place it by the side of the fire to simmer for three minutes, after which take it out and cut it in halves; taste it in order to ascertain if it be correctly seasoned, and see that when cut asunder, the inner part presents a smooth, light, compact surface.

Quenelle was a delicate forcemeat made from a combination of finely ground meat and a bread or flour paste called *panada*. It was also made from fish. A fine fat, usually calf's udder, or butter was added to ensure succulence. This paste could be used to stuff small birds or profiteroles for soup (see recipe 157). But usually it was formed into small dumplings called quenelles. These were often served in consommé. They were often formed between two teaspoons, though there were also purpose-made quenelle molds. To make a basic flour paste panada, boil half a pint of stock with two ounces of butter and a pinch of salt. Bring these to the boil and stir in four large tablespoons of white flour, stirring constantly until it forms a delicate paste and starts to come away from the sides of the pan. Let it cool before you use it. Calf's udder is a fat that it is attached to the inner part of a leg of veal. It is almost impossible to obtain, so use butter instead.

❧ 164. DUCK IN THE PIEDMONT MANNER ❧

Italy (Lombardy) 1829. (Luraschi, 85)

Clean the duck, bone it, then put it in the right sized casserole, with a bunch of parsley, onion, cloves of garlic, two cloves, thyme, bay leaf, basil, a handful of coriander, a piece of butter, two glasses of stock and one of white wine, cook on a gentle fire, when the duck feels cooked under the finger, pass the sauce through a sieve, degrease, then reduce on the stove and serve on bread crostini fried in butter.

You may be able to persuade your butcher or game dealer to bone you a duck. If not, use a whole one. A wild duck like a mallard would be the most suitable for this dish as they are not as fat as most domestic breeds. It would have been cooked over charcoal in a saucepan, probably with extra coals on the lid. If you have one, use a small dutch oven. To make the crostini, fry some slices of good quality white bread in some butter in a frying pan.

❧ 165. HUNTER'S HARE ❧

Italy (Lombardy) 1829. (Luraschi, 143)

Take an already cleansed hare, cut into small pieces, cut into slices five or six large onions, put in a casserole with two ounces of butter, let the onions and butter brown, unite them with the hare and make them cook together, moisten with a glass of Malaga, or Madeira, or Marsala wine, put in salt, pepper and a slice of ham, cover well, and cook on a low fire. At the end of cooking add a glass of coulis or gravy, degrease it, pour it on the plate with a border of pastry and serve it.

These rich, highly flavored stews were popular in northern Italy. This one must be cooked very slowly with a tightly sealed lid on the saucepan. The onions cook down to a delicious purée. It was served on a metal plate that had a collar of cooked puff pastry baked on its rim. In Italian this was described as a *bordo di pasta*, but this does not mean a border of pasta of the macaroni variety. Before the tureen became widespread in Europe, soups and stews were often served on plates that had a border of puff pastry baked on them. It acted as a kind of reservoir that stopped the juices from overflowing.

FISH

❧ 166. TURBOT SALAD ❧

France 1814. (Beauvilliers, vol. 2, 46)

Take turbot that has remained from a former day and skin it; cut it in any form, round, long, or fan shaped; dish it as a crown; garnish it with stripes of anchovies, capers, truffles, and beet root; fill up the interstices with lettuce, and every other salad vegetable in their season; make a sauce of oil, vinegar, salt, and pepper, and serve it.

This type of salad has an interesting history. It was first described in 1662 in the anonymous *l'Escole parfaite des officiers de bouche*, where it was called a *sallade couronnèe*—a crowned salad. However, in this earlier version, a crown-shaped border was cut from slices of citron peel rather than pieces of fish. The citron peel crown enclosed a decorative salad of lettuce, lemon slices, pomegranate seeds, and almonds. The author gives detailed instructions on how to make crowns suitable for serving to a king, a prince, a duke, a marquis, and a count, all fashioned in the correct form. A royal crown had to be surmounted by little citron peel fleur-de-lies on the tips, while a prince's had a mixture of fleur-de-lies and trefoils.[2] If you have some cold, leftover turbot or other firm white fish, you might like to attempt Beauvilliers's crown-shaped border and decorate it artistically with anchovies, pieces of beetroot, and capers. Beauvilliers once worked for Louis XVI's brother, who eventually became Louis XVIII, so he may have made this kind of salad when he worked in the prince's household. Shapes cut from prunes have the same dark color as truffles. If you sprinkle your salad with a little truffle oil as well as the dressing, you might also fool your guests into believing that you have used real truffles.

⭐ 167. COLLARED SALMON ⭐

England 1816. (Hammond, 48)

Split enough of the fish to form a handsome roll, wash, and wipe it; then, having previously mixed a sufficient quantity of white pepper, pounded mace, salt, and Jamaica pepper, to season it highly, rub it inside and out well; after which roll it tight and bandage it; put as much water and one third vinegar as will cover it, with salt, bay leaves, and both sorts of pepper; then cover it close, and simmer it till done enough. Drain and boil quick the liquor, which put on when cold; serve with fennel. This forms an elegant dish, and may be esteemed as a peculiar delicacy.

Collaring was usually a way of preserving fish or meat by keeping it in souse or pickle. However, this particular dish was designed to be served to table as soon as it had cooled. Because collared fish was boiled, it was tightly wrapped in a cloth to stop it from disintegrating. After cooling down, the fish became firm and the bandage or cloth was carefully removed. Once the salmon had been taken out, the cooking liquid was reduced and used as a sauce. This is what is meant by boiling it "quick." Use a full side of salmon, rub in the seasonings—Jamaica pepper is allspice—and then roll it up into a tight spiral. Tie it in a cotton or linen cloth and secure this with tape rather than string.

⅊ 168. COD ALLA ROBERTA ⅌

Italy (Lombardy) 1829. (Luraschi, 416)

Brown in butter an onion chopped into little cubes, put in a little sauce, a little coulis, salt and pepper, then put in the cod skinned and boned, take up to a careful simmer on a gentle fire and serve with crostini as you please.

With its flavoring of coulis, this very simple recipe shows the strong French influence on northern Italian cookery. If you want try to make it, use the sauce in recipe 178 and the coulis in Recipe 133. Crostini were made by frying pieces of bread in butter, or rubbing them with butter and grilling them over the coals on a gridiron.

⅊ 169. SWEET AND SOUR COD ⅌

Italy (Lombardy) 1829. (Luraschi, 416)

Clean a fillet of cod, cut into pieces, roll in flour, fry in boiling oil, pile up on the plate, pour on it a sweet-sour salsa, sprinkle with breadcrumbs and toast with a salamander and serve.

This basic fried cod dish is served with a sweet-sour salsa that contains raisins and pine nuts (see Recipe 179). The dish is a remarkable survival of a medieval favorite known in the fourteenth century as fish *egre-douce*, illustrating that the powerful influence of French cuisine could not completely eradicate all vestiges of the old cooking style.

⅊ 170. HERRING SALAD ⅌

*Germany (Cologne) 1846. (*Kleine kölner köchin, *163)*

Leave the herring to stand for 2 hours in water, then skin and bone the fish, cut into small pieces, place these on a plate, adding finely chopped onions and apples, finely minced cold meat, capers and pepper and mix with oil and vinegar. If the herring has a roe, mash it with oil and vinegar and add to the herring.

This dish has survived into modern times as the well-known Berlin herring salad. However, in this early version from Cologne, minced cold meat is included in the ingredients. Use finely chopped veal or chicken.

⅊ 171. CRAYFISH BUTTER ⅌

England 1846. (Francatelli, 42)

Remove the shells from three or four dozen crayfish, place them on a baking-sheet in the oven to dry; let the shells cool, pound them in a mortar, with a little lobster coral and four ounces of fresh butter; thoroughly bruise the whole well together, so as to form them into a kind of paste, put this into a stew pan, and then set it on the stove-fire to simmer for about five minutes; then rub it through a tammy with considerable pressure into a basin containing some cold water, with a piece of ice in it; as soon as the colored crayfish butter is become set, through the coldness of the water, take it out, and put it into a small basin in a cool place till wanted for use.

This rose-colored butter was a favorite dressing for fish and was an important ingredient in some poultry-based recipes like Antonin Carême's profiterole soup à la Wagram (recipe 157). You can also make a similar butter with prawn or shrimp shells. Lobster coral was the name given to the bright red roe or eggs that are sometimes found clustered underneath the bodies of cooked hen lobsters. They were an important garnish at this period.

❧ 172. POTTED SALMON ❧

England 1847. (Robinson, 33)

Take a salmon, split it at the back and through the belly, making two separate sides of it. Scale it very clean, and wipe it, but do not let water come near it. Lay fine salt upon it, letting it lie until melted away from it; then take pepper, mace, cloves, and a little brown sugar, which rub all over the red side, and then with a few bay leaves (cut in pieces) put it into a pan, with plenty of butter, out of which the salt has been washed, to bake in a slow oven. When it is done, let the gravy be poured away, and take out the fish, lay it on a clean cloth to drain, put it into your pots, press it as close down as you possibly can, and pour clarified butter over it.

Potted meats and fish were important preserved foods that could be kept for months in a cool larder. They predate canning and bottling by many hundreds of years. After cooking, but before it could cool, the flesh was pushed down into little glazed ceramic pots and the surface was sealed with a layer of clarified butter. This kept the air out and prevented spoilage. The salting process and the addition of spices also helped to preserve the fish or meat. To make clarified butter, melt some unsalted butter in a small saucepan. Do not let it boil. Skim off any solids floating on top and allow the sediment to settle—this is a combination of water and milk solids. Carefully decant the clear oily butter and discard the solids left in the saucepan. Pour this over your potted salmon.

VEGETABLES

❧ 173. SAVOYARD POTATO FRITTERS ❧

Italy (Lombardy) 1829. (Luraschi, 388)

Cook in water six potatoes, peel and pound them in a mortar, mix with two ounces of sugar, a little cinnamon, three ounces of fresh butter, three egg yolks, a little candied citron minced fine, mix everything together, remove from the mortar, make it into little pieces the size of a walnut, dust with flour and shape with your hand into the form of sausages, fry in clarified butter in a tart pan and serve.

With their flavoring of candied citron and cinnamon, these unusual sweetened potato fritters are reminiscent of a much earlier style of Italian cookery. They were probably dusted with powdered sugar just before serving.

Savory Pastries

❧ 174. YORKSHIRE, OR CHRISTMAS PIE ☙

England 1846. (Francatelli, 383)

First, bone a turkey, a goose, a brace of young pheasants, four partridges, four woodcocks, a dozen snipes, four grouse, and four widgeons; then boil and trim a small York ham and two tongues. Season and garnish the inside of the fore-named game and poultry, as directed in the foregoing case, with long fillets of fat bacon and tongue, and French truffles; each must be carefully sewn up with a needle and small twine, so as to prevent the force-meat from escaping while they are being baked. When the whole of these are ready, line two round or oval braising-pans with thin layers of fat bacon, and after the birds have been arranged therein in neat order, and covered in with layers of bacon and buttered paper, put the lids on, and set them in the oven to bake rather slowly, for about four hours: then withdraw them, and allow them to cool.

While the foregoing is in progress, prepare some highly-seasoned aspic-jelly with the carcasses of the game and poultry, to which add six calves'-feet, and the usual complement of vegetables, &c., and when done, let it be clarified: one-half should be reduced previously to its being poured into the pie when it is baked.

Make about sixteen pounds of hot-water-paste, and use it to raise a pie of sufficient dimensions to admit of its holding the game and poultry prepared for the purpose, for making which follow the directions contained in the foregoing article. The inside of the pie must first be lined with thin layers of fat bacon, over which spread a coating of well-seasoned force-meat of fat livers; the birds should then be placed in the following order: first, put the goose at the bottom with some of the small birds round it, filling up the cavities with some of the force-meat; then, put the turkey and the pheasants with thick slices of the boiled ham between them, reserving the woodcocks and widgeons, that these may be placed on the top: fill the cavities with force-meat and truffles, and cover the whole with thin layers of fat bacon, run a little plain melted butter over the surface, cover the pie in the usual manner, and ornament it with a bold design. The pie must now be baked, for about six hours, in an oven moderately heated, and when taken out, and after the reduced aspic above alluded to has been poured into it, stop the hole up with a small piece of paste, and set it aside in the larder to become cold.

Queen Victoria's Yorkshire Christmas pie.

Note.—*The quantity of game, &c., recommended to be used in the preparation of the foregoing pie may appear extravagant enough, but it is to be remembered that these very large pies are mostly in request at Christmas time. Their substantial aspect renders them worthy of appearing on the side-table of those wealthy epicures who are wont to keep up the good old English style, at this season of hospitality and good cheer.*

Like Carême's boar's head, the recipe for this festival pie has been included here as an interesting example of nineteenth-century extravagance. With its foie gras forcemeat (referred to here as fat livers), truffles, and game, this would be an expensive and technically difficult dish to replicate in a modern kitchen. These pies had been made in northern England since at least the eighteenth century and were often given as gifts. They were filled with a variety of boned birds, one inside the other like a Russian doll, and were often elegantly decorated. In 1857 one was served for Christmas dinner at Windsor Castle that was so large that four footmen were required to carry it to the Queen's table. In a contemporary newspaper account of the event it was remarked, "The Christmas Pie is a most important affair, of huge dimensions, and its work is of no slight difficulty, not only as far as its ornamentation is concerned, but also as regards cooking such an immense mass of comestibles."[3] Francatelli's recipe differs from some of the more traditional recipes of the previous century. The inclusion of truffles and goose livers shows that this is an adaptation of the dish created by a master chef trained in the Anglo-French culinary system. He also precooks the fowl in order to ensure that this enormous mass of "comestibles" is cooked all of the way through to the center. The pastry decorations were frequently stamped out of skillfully carved molds called "boards."

⊰ 175. HOT WATER PASTE FOR RAISED PIES ⊱

England 1846. (Francatelli, 387)

INGREDIENTS:—*One pound of flour, four ounces of butter, a teaspoonful of salt, about a gill and a half of hot water.*

Place the flour on the pastry-table, spread it out with the back of the hand, so as to form a well or hollow in the centre, into this put the salt. Next, put the butter and water into a stew pan over the fire, and when they are sufficiently heated, so that one can just bear the finger in, pour them both gradually in upon the flour, and mix them quickly together with the hand, taking particular care to knead the whole firmly, and at once, into a compact paste: then press this smoothly together in a napkin, and afterwards keep it covered up in stew pan in a warm place till used.

This makes a very strong durable pastry for raised pies, like that in the previous recipe and the lumber pie (recipe 60). Some bakers mixed the ingredients together in a large bowl using the end of a rolling pin—a sensible precaution, because this pastry can cause burns. When it became comfortable to handle, it was worked on a slab. One way of making or raising a pie "coffin" was to use the hands to mold the pastry into a cone shape on a sheet of floured paper. The top of the cone was cut off with a sharp knife and reserved for making the lid. The fingers of one hand were then pushed down into the center of the truncated cone to create a hollow. The pastry mass was then rotated on the paper and the coffin formed in the same way that you might make a pot. Once it was evenly formed it was filled and the lid stuck on with water or egg yolk. The seams at the top were then welded together with a pastry crimper.

SAUCES

◁3 176. GREEN SAUCE FOR DUCKLINGS AND GREEN GEESE ▷

England 1801. (Mollard, 268)

Pick green spinach or sorrel, wash it, and bruise it in a marble mortar, and strain the liquor through a tamis cloth. To a gill of the juice add a little loaf sugar, the yolk of a raw egg, and a spoonful of vinegar; if spinach juice, then put one ounce of fresh butter, and whisk all together over a fire till it begins to boil. N. B. Should the sauce be made of spinach juice instead of vinegar, there may be put two table spoonfuls of the pulp of gooseberries rubbed through a hair sieve.

This acidic green sauce dates back to the medieval period. It was very popular for serving with fatty foods like duck and geese. A "green goose" was a young bird, usually a male surplus to requirements, that was fattened up and killed for the table, usually in late May or June. This was the time that gooseberries were in season in England and there is a theory that gooseberries got their name because they were used for making this particular sauce. However, this is probably just a nice myth, as an early name for the fruit is *groser* or *grosberry*, derived from the French name *groseille*. It is easier nowadays to liquidize the sorrel or spinach leaves in a food processor and squeeze the juice out in a muslin cloth.

❧ 177. BEEF JUS ❧

France 1814. (Beauvilliers, vol. 1, 32)

Butter the bottom of a stew pan, put into it some thin slices of ham and lard or bacon, with slices of onions and carrots, covering the whole with thick slices of beef, wet it with two spoonfuls of grand bouillon, or good stock, make it boil upon a brisk fire; when it begins to stick, give it a prick with a knife; put it upon a slow fire or furnace, and take care it does not burn; when it is firmly fixed, wet it as directed for the blond de veau, skim it and season it with a bunch of parsley, and some stalks of mushrooms; when the meat is sufficiently cooked take off the fat and run the juice through a napkin; make use of it to color potages, sauces, or made-dishes, which either require jus or coloring.

Originally beef jus was the gravy that naturally flowed from spit-roasted meats. It was often in short supply, so this recipe was designed to create larger quantities of this important flavoring. Jus was a stock ingredient of many recipes. *Blond de veau* was a similar preparation made from veal rather than beef. In Beauvilliers's recipe for *blond de veau,* he wets the meat when it has stuck to the bottom of the pan with a good quantity of strong-flavored bouillon.

❧ 178. SIMPLE ITALIAN SALSA ❧

Italy (Lombardy) 1829. (Luraschi, 335)

Melt on the stove a piece of butter with a little chopped shallot and a clove of garlic and add some little mushrooms chopped fine, wet with a little white wine and a little coulis, add a half lemon without its skin cut in slices, let it cook for an hour, degrease and pass through a sieve and serve on entrees of braised poultry.

Luraschi also gives a recipe for a *salsa vera d'Italia*—authentic Italian salsa—the main difference being the inclusion of a whole truffle. Compared to the *salse* and *sapore* of earlier Italian cookbooks, this sauce shows the extent to which French cuisine had modified sauce recipes in Italy.

❧ 179. SWEET-SOUR SALSA ❧

Italy (Lombardy) 1829. (Luraschi, 340)

Put in a saucepan four ounces of sugar and cook it to a very light brown, wet it with a glass of vinegar, add a little lemon peel, reduce it a little and strain it through a napkin, transfer to a clean casserole with an ounce of raisins and an ounce of clean pine nuts, let it boil and it serves for broiled neck of veal.

With its inclusion of pine nuts and raisins and sweet-sour flavor, this preparation is more reminiscent of medieval and Renaissance cuisine. To make the caramel, put two teaspoons of lemon juice and four ounces of sugar in a saucepan and stir them until the sugar completely dissolves. Allow it to boil without stirring and instantly remove from the heat when the sugar starts to turn a very light brown. Plunge the saucepan into cold water to stop the sugar from cooking any more. Allow it to cool for a few minutes and stir in a wine glass of balsamic vinegar. Add the lemon peel. Return it to the heat to thicken it a little. Strain out the lemon peel and mix with the chopped pine nuts and raisins. Serve with sweet and sour cod, recipe 169.

⠦ 180. PINE NUT SALSA ALLA CERTOSINA ⠴

Italy (Lombardy) 1829. (Luraschi, 341)

Grind three ounces of pine nuts in a little water, rub through a sieve, put to it a little salt, a little pepper and dissolve in a little good oil and a little vinegar and it serves for cold fowl.

The small town of Certosa in Lombardy gets its name from the nearby Certosa di Pavia, an impressive Carthusian monastery. Certosa in Italian means a charterhouse or Carthusian community. This sauce may have originated in the locality, though the best pine nuts were said to come from the Adriatic coast in the vicinity of Ravenna.

⠦ 181. CREAM BÉCHAMEL SAUCE ⠴

England 1846. (Francatelli, 3)

Put six ounces of fresh butter into a middle-sized stew pan; add four ounces of sifted flour, some nutmeg, a few peppercorns, and a little salt; knead the whole well together; then cut one carrot and one onion into very thin slices, throw them into the stew pan, and also a bouquet of parsley, thyme, and half a bay-leaf, tied together; next moisten these with a quart of white broth and a pint of cream; and having stirred the sauce over the stove fire for about half an hour, pass it through the tammy into a basin for use. This sauce is not expensive, neither does it require much time or trouble to make. It is very useful as a substitute for velouté, or other white sauces, as also for many other purposes, as will be shown hereafter.

A classic béchamel was based on a velouté sauce that had been diluted with cream. Velouté is still one of the two stock sauces used as foundation for making many other French sauces. The other is espagnole, or brown sauce. Both these were made in enormous quantities in professional kitchens. However, velouté and espagnole, as they were made at the time of Carême and Francatelli, would be very time consuming and impractical to make today. This "quick" béchamel is much closer to the trimmed-down modern version of the sauce. However, the quantities given here were designed for professional use.

Starches and Pastas

ᴥ 182. PELOE OF RICE ᴥ

England 1801. (Mollard, 96)

Wash and pick two pounds of rice, boil it in plenty of water till half done, with a dozen of whole cardamom seeds, then drain it, pick out the seeds, put the rice into a stew pan, with three quarters of a pound of fresh butter and some pounded mace, and salt to the palate. Take a loin of house lamb or some fresh pork cut into small pieces; put them into a frying-pan, add cinnamon, cloves, cumin and cardamom seeds, a small quantity of each pounded and sifted, with a bit of butter and some cayenne pepper, and fry the meat till half done. Then take two bay leaves, four good-sized onions sliced, and add to them a pint and a half of veal stock. Boil them till tender and rub them through a tamis cloth or sieve; then boil the liquor over a fire till it is reduced to half a pint, add it to the fried meat and spices, together with some peeled button onions boiled. Then put some of the rice at the bottom of another stew pan, then a layer of meat and onions on the rice, and so on alternately till the whole is put in. Cover the pan close, set it in a moderately heated oven for two hours and a half, and when it is to be served up turn the rice out carefully on a dish.

This is an interesting British attempt to replicate an oriental pilaf. The use of freshly ground spices is noteworthy. Later Victorian curries and pilafs utilized commercially produced curry powder. This recipe makes a delicious layered dish of rice and lamb.

ᴥ 183. GNOCCHI ALLA MILANESE ᴥ

Italy (Lombardy) 1829. (Luraschi, 113)

Take a pound of pasta flour, put it in a large bowl with a pinch of powdered salt, some spice, a little pepper, two soldi of bread grated and sifted, three ounces of grana cheese and three eggs, mix all these with tepid water and beat the dough well with a wooden spoon, watch out that it is not too liquid, but rather firm. Make it into a paste. Take some thin or weak stock, boil this in a large pan, and with a silver spoon form the gnocchi one at a time of the size you wish, it is usual that they are a half spoon each; put them in the boiling stock, cook them for half an hour, when cooked remove with the skimmer, and drain on a sieve. Dress with purified butter and finely grated cheese and serve in a silver tureen, or one in the fashion of silver, or on a plate with a border of paste, and if you please pour a sostanza on top and serve.

These gnocchi were molded with a silver teaspoon, rather like quenelles. A quicker method is to roll the paste out into long sausages about half an inch in thickness and to cut them into quarter-inch lengths on a floured wooden board with a sharp knife. Mix in three ounces of grana padana cheese. Use a little ground nutmeg and black pepper for the spice. A soldo was a small denomination coin like a penny or cent, so "two soldi" means two cents worth of bread, a quantity impossible to determine, but 16 ounces of breadcrumbs works well for the quantity above. After the egg has been blended in, it only takes a little tepid water to make a pliable paste. Purified butter is clarified butter (see recipe 172). Most modern gnocchi, like those based on potato,

Making gnocchi or quenelles with two spoons.

only need a few minutes cooking time. These gnocchi really do need to be gently boiled for 30 minutes or they will taste a bit raw. These rather substantial little dumplings are related to the *knödeln* of neighboring Austria. A *sostanza* is an old Milanese name for a sauce or coulis.

⨟ 184. PETITES FONDUES AU PÂTE D'ITALIE ⨠

England 1846. (Soyer, 581)

Blanch a quarter of a pound of any description of Italian paste in boiling water a few minutes, strain it upon a silk sieve until a little dry, put an ounce of butter and a spoonful of flour, mix well together, then add half a pint of boiling milk; stir over the fire until thickish, add your paste, stir it a few minutes longer over the fire, then add a quarter of a pound of Stilton cheese in small lumps, and a quarter of a pound of grated Parmesan; season with a little pepper, salt, and cayenne, add six yolks of eggs, stir it another minute until the eggs are partially set, and when cold whip the whites very stiff; mix them well in, fill small paper cases with it, bake a quarter of an hour in a moderate oven, and serve very hot.

These little savories look like cheese muffins or miniature soufflés. Use short macaroni, fusilli, or conchiglie pasta shapes. Cook the pasta according to the manufacturer's instructions or until it is *al dente*—firm between the teeth. It is important to allow the sauce to cool completely before carefully folding in the beaten egg whites a little at a time. Quickly spoon the mixture in to paper muffin cases. Cook them according to the recipe. They must be served immediately. This is a typical Anglo-French use of an Italian ingredient.

PUDDINGS

⨟ 185. SPINACH PUDDING ⨠

Germany (Hamburg) 1803. (Die sich selbst lehrende köchin, 219)

Boil and shred the spinach, add breadcrumbs, minced kidney fat, raisins, currants, nutmeg, and eggs, the whites of which have been whipped, and a little sweet top of the milk. Mix well, then tie the mixture in a pudding cloth and boil. As it is difficult to weigh spinach accurately, use your own judgment about all quantities, reckoning 3 eggs for every two persons.

It is sometimes said that the English were alone in making suet puddings. Here is evidence that they were also made in Germany. Suet is the firm crumbly fat found surrounding the animal's kidneys. "Sweet top of milk" means cream. The only sweetener in this interesting pudding is provided by the dried fruit. It is likely that a sweet sauce was poured over it.

☜ 186. TURBAN OF APPLES ☞

Anglo-French 1813. (Ude, 413)

Take some real reinettes, cut them into oval quarters, and stew them in some thin syrup. Mind they do not break. You have boiled some rice in cream, with a little lemon, sugar and salt. Let the rice be well done thoroughly and kept thick. Then let it cool. When it is nearly cold, take a large piece of bread, or rather an empty gallipot, which you put in the centre of your dish, and lay your rice all around till you reach the top of the gallipot. You next take your pieces of apples that have been drained of all the syrup through a sieve, and thrust them into the rice, sloping towards the right in the first row, and towards the left in the second, and so on till you reach the top of your turban, which you put into the oven that the apples may be made of a fine color. When you are ready to serve up, you remove the gallipot, wipe all the butter, which may occasionally be about the middle of the dish, and pour in a creme patissière, that is made as follows.

Both savory and sweet dishes arranged in the shape of turbans were very popular at this period and made good table centerpieces. This is one of the easier ones to make. You will need a good quantity of cold, thick, well-cooked rice. Use a short-grained pudding rice variety that will become sticky and glutinous when cold. Cook it in light cream with sugar and lemon zest. When it is completely cool, sculpt it on a dish around a tall, well-buttered jam jar (a *gallipot* was a ceramic jar) in the shape of an oriental turban. Starting at the base of your rice turban, gently push a row of quarter apple pieces into the rice, making sure they lean to the right. Arrange another row orientated to the left and continue alternating the rows until you come to the top. Brush over the turban with a little melted butter. Bake in a hot oven until the apples become a lovely golden color. Let it cool a little and then carefully rotate the jam jar to loosen it. Pull it out with a twisting movement and fill the void with the crème pâtissiere in the next recipe. Ornament your turban with shapes cut out of candied orange, lemon, and citron peels and glace cherries.

Reinette apples are a type of pippin. A number of varieties are still grown in France, the most revered being *la Reine de Reinette*—or "little queen of queens." They keep well and have a good sweet flavor. If you cannot get hold of a true Reinette variety use a sweet eating apple like a Newtown Pippin or Cox's Orange Pippin. Avoid sharp-flavored cooking apples, which tend to disintegrate quickly into a purée. Stew the carefully quartered apples in syrup made of two pints of water and a half pound of sugar.

◈ 187. CRÈME PATISSIÈRE FOR THE TURBAN OF APPLES ◈

Anglo-French 1813. (Ude, 413)

Take a pint of cream and a pint of milk, boil them and keep stirring with a spoon. When the cream has boiled, add to it about two ounces of sugar, a little salt, and the peel of a lemon. Let this peel diffuse till the cream tastes of the lemon; you next beat the yolks of eight eggs with the cream, and do them on the fire, stirring all the while with a wooden spoon. When the cream is got very thick you pour it into a hair sieve to drain, and keep pressing upon it with your wooden spoon. When entirely strained, you put it in a pan to serve you when wanted. If you wish your crème patissière to be very thick, you must have more eggs to it. After having poured the cream inside of your turban; you must ornament it with sweetmeats of various colors.

◈ 188. CHARLOTTE OF APPLES ◈

France 1828. (Carême, 212)

Clean and cut in small quarters twenty-four apples; sauté them in a large stew-pan, with four ounces of butter and four ounces of sugar on which the rind of an orange or Seville orange has been rubbed; the apples covered, over a slow fire, stirring them from time to time, till they may be equally done, but yet remain as whole as possible; mix with them a pot of fine cherries, drained from their syrup; during their boiling, cut the crumb of a loaf a day old, in strips half an inch wide, dip these columns in four ounces of butter, simply melted, and range them in the mould so as to cover the bottom and sides; pour apples into the Charlotte, and cover the top with a slice of crumb dipped in butter; three-quarters of an hour before serving, put it in a quick oven, or else on some red cinders, surrounding it with small live-burning coals; after half an hour's baking, observe if it be of a fine light brown color, and if so, turn it out on to the dish, if not, renew the fire; when done, take off the mould, and cover it slightly with a brush with apricot jam, or apple or currant jelly, or with the syrup of the cherries; the mould must be well buttered before using: some glaze the mould with pounded sugar, but it is preferable without, as the charlotte thus becomes sometimes of a deeper color in one place than another.

You will need a charlotte mold or a deep cake tin to make this excellent sweet *entremet*. Carême's directions are for a very large charlotte, so adjust

Apple charlotte and charlotte mold.

the number of apples and other ingredients according to the size of your mold. The best bread for making the columns is a dense white loaf that has been left a day or two to firm up. Cut strips exactly half an inch wide and the same length as the internal height of your mold—after dipping them in the butter, arrange them in the mold. Bake it in a hot oven. The strips of bread will fry against the side of the hot copper mold and should be crisp when cooked. Invert the mold on a plate and carefully tip the charlotte out. Dissolve a couple of tablespoons of apricot jam in a tablespoon of water in a saucepan and use this to glaze the outside of the charlotte. Carême mixed a few preserved cherries with the apples, while other authors included apricots or quinces.

❧ 189. BLACK BREAD PUDDING ❧

Germany (Cologne) 1846. (Kleine kölner köchin, 137)

Take two slices of black bread, the width of the entire loaf and as thick as three fingers, make into breadcrumbs and place in half a measure of red wine. Stir together 10 egg yolks with some butter, cinnamon, some crushed cloves, sufficient sugar and a few raisins to form a soft paste, adding the soaked bread and the wine bit by bit. Whip the whites of the 10 eggs until stiff, then fold these into the bread mixture and place the resultant dough in a basin greased with butter and sprinkled with biscuit crumbs. Cover the basin tightly and stand in boiling water for two hours. In the meantime make the following sauce: set half a measure of red wine on the heat, with a cinnamon stick, sufficient sugar and a few slices of lemon. Beat together the whites of two eggs and the yolks of six, stir into the wine and bring to the boil a few times.

This unusual pudding is made from black rye bread. If you cannot get any true black bread, use a dark sourdough rye, but you will not get quite the same effect. The two slices cut "thick as three fingers" are about two inches thick.

CAKES AND BREADS

❧ 190. TWELFTH CAKES ❧

England 1801. (Mollard, 286)

Take seven pounds of flour, make a cavity in the center, set a sponge with a gill and a half of yeast and a little warm milk; then put round it one pound of fresh butter broke into small lumps, one pound and a quarter of sifted sugar, four pounds and a half of currants washed and picked, half an ounce of sifted cinnamon, a quarter of an ounce of pounded cloves, mace, and nutmeg mixed, sliced candied orange or lemon peel and citron. When the sponge is risen, mix all the ingredients together with a little warm milk; let the hoops be well papered and buttered, then fill them with the mixture and bake them, and when nearly cold ice them over with sugar prepared for that purpose as per receipt; or they may be plain.

Although the tradition of making these cakes dates back to the medieval period, this seems to be the earliest printed recipe for an English twelfth cake. These decorated cakes were an important element in the celebrations for the feast of the Epiphany on the sixth of January. They were at the height of their popularity when Mollard wrote his cookbook. It was the custom for each guest at a Twelfth Day entertainment at this time to take on the role of a particular character for the whole evening. This was achieved by choosing a card at random from a pack. These were illustrated with images of various comic characters. As well as the King and Queen of the Bean, who led the revels, there were many others—Counselor Double Fee, Mrs. Prittle Prattle, the Duchess of Puddle Dock, and Sir Tun Belly Wash were all popular. The evening's entertainment ended with the finale of cutting the elegantly iced cake, which was usually very large and decorated with two crowns for the king and queen and sugar paste or wax images of the other characters.

⍍ 191. TO BAKE A STOLLEN ⍰

Germany (Hamburg) 1803. (Die sich selbst lehrende köchin, 6)

Take one measure of milk, one and a half pounds of good butter, 2 pounds of large and half a pound of small raisins, a quarter of a pound of almonds, 2 loth of candied lemon peel, 4 loth of sugar, 2 eggs, good yeast and sufficient fine wheat flour to make into a fairly stiff dough. Put the flour in a trough, heat the milk until the butter melts in it, pour into the flour along with the yeast, stir in the other ingredients, mix together to form a fairly stiff dough and leave to stand for a good hour to rise. Then shape the dough into a stollen or roll, according to whether you want them large or small. When formed, leave to rise a little longer, then send them to the baker's. As soon as they come out of the oven, brush with rose water and melted butter, then sprinkle with sugar and cinnamon.

This traditional German Christmas bread probably started life in fifteenth-century Dresden, though these very early versions were very basic and contained no fruit or sugar. In 1730 it is alleged that Augustus II of Saxony fed over 20,000 Dresden citizens with a 1.5-ton stollen made by the city's bakers' guild. This early nineteenth-century recipe from Hamburg is rich in butter and dried fruit, but unlike modern versions, is not very sweet and contains no marzipan. This is probably because it was eaten with wine. A *loth* was about half an ounce. A Hamburg measure was a wine measure, roughly equivalent to a modern quart. By small raisins is meant currants. If you want to replicate this old stollen recipe using the quantities above, you will need a little over ten pounds of flour. This is enough to make 16 good-sized stollen, so you might prefer to quarter the quantities. Because the dough is very butter-rich, it can take much longer to rise than indicated in the recipe. When the dough has doubled in size, knock it down and divide it into equal portions and form them into a long rectangular stollen shape. Allow them to rise further and bake them at about 375°F for about 40 minutes.

❧ 192. ROUT CAKES ☙

Scotland 1809. (Caird, 162)

Flour, 1 pound. Sugar, 8 ounces.
   Pounded Almonds, 4 ounces. The yolks of 8 Eggs.
   Cast the sugar and eggs light, then add the flour and almonds, pour it into a tablet frame or sheet of paper buttered, with the edges an inch turned up and twisted; then spread equally with a knife. When fired, make icing with some fine sugar and the white of egg, it may be either white or colored; lay it over the bottom of the cake, and with a sharp knife cut them in various shapes; they are then ornamented with nonpareils, &c.

A rout was a fashionable entertainment, not a riotous assembly. These little iced cakes were very popular and are mentioned in Jane Austen's novel *Emma* (1816). Caird's remarkably detailed book gives us an excellent insight into the skills of a late-Georgian confectioner. He was a native of Edinburgh, so he uses some Scottish terms—*to cast* is to beat eggs, while *to fire* means to bake. If you bake the cake in a paper case, brush the paper all over with a wet pastry brush after you have taken it out of the oven. This will enable you to remove the cake with ease. Caird's book seems to be one of the first in the English language to list the ingredients at the beginning of the recipe.

❧ 193. MADELEINES ☙

France 1814. (Beauvilliers, vol. 2, 134)

Break ten eggs; keep the whites and yolks separate; add to the yolks three quarters of a pound of sifted sugar; a little minced lemon peel and salt: beat the whole together as for biscuit; put in half a pound of flour, and mix; add half a pound of clarified butter; whip six whites of eggs, till they are firm; mix them lightly in; butter small Madeleine moulds or any other; fill them with the paste; bake them in a slow oven; they take more baking than biscuit: in default of small moulds make it like a cake in a paper case; cut it down, and serve.

Tablet or biscuit frame.

These little cakes are still baked in fluted molds that resemble a scallop shell. They were made famous by Marcel Proust in *À la recherche du temps perdu (Remembrance of Things Past,* 1913), in which the narrator is transported back in time by the evocative smell and taste of a madeleine dipped in lime flower tea. This recipe dates from nearly a hundred years before Proust's nostalgic episode. Like a lot of early recipes this is intended for a large quantity. Half the quantities will still make a good amount. Traditional madeleine molds can still be obtained. If you cannot get hold of some, take the author's advice and bake the mixture in a cake pan. Beat the egg yolks and sugar for quite a long time to aerate them. Gently fold in a little flower at a time with a wooden spoon. Make sure the melted butter is cool but still liquid. Before you start to add it to the mixture, fold in a little of beaten egg white to lighten the butter. Fold it into the batter. Then, in three stages, gently fold the egg white into the mixture.

SWEET PASTRIES

⊰ 194. FINE SPONGATI ITALIAN CAKE ⊱

Anglo-Italian 1820. (Jarrin, 161)

One pound six ounces of white bread, dried in the oven and reduced to a coarse powder; one pound four ounces of walnuts, blanched, and chopped very fine with a double handled knife; six ounces of currants, well washed and cleaned; five ounces of wild pine kernels; five pounds five ounces of virgin honey, clarified; three grains of cinnamon in powder, one grain of cloves; one grain of strong pepper; and one grain of nutmeg in powder. The above articles must be mixed together, and enclosed in a crust paste, made of the following materials, viz., two pounds eight ounces of the best wheaten flour; six ounces of fresh butter; five ounces of loaf sugar, pounded; one ounce of olive oil, of Aix, in Provence, and half an ounce of salt, with a sufficient quantity of white wine to mix the whole. This paste, being of a moderate consistence, is to be formed into round cases or crusts, into which the first mixture is to be introduced, and a cover of the same paste must be put on, which must be pricked all over with the point of the knife. Let them stand for a whole day, put them in an oven, moderately heated, on plates dusted over with flour: these cakes should be an inch thick; they may be iced or not, as you please.

This remarkable recipe is for *spongata,* a traditional Christmas pastry from Emilia-Romagna in northern Italy. The cake, which is rather like a British mince pie, is still made in a number of villages and towns in the vicinity of Parma. It varies considerably from place to place and a lot of bakers and families keep their recipes closely guarded secrets. Although the *spongata* is a very ancient cake, it would appear that the earliest printed recipe is this one of Jarrin's, which was published in London in 1820. He came from the town of Colorno near Parma but ran various confectionery shops in London for most of his life. He was famous for his beautifully decorated twelfth cakes. It would be nice to think that he also sold his native *spongata* cakes to Londoners during the festive season.

⚱ 195. GERMAN TOURTE OF APRICOTS ⚱

England 1846. (Francatelli, 421)

Cut a dozen ripe apricots into quarters, and put them into a small sugar-boiler or stew pan, with the kernels extracted from the stones, four ounces of pounded sugar, and a spoonful of water; stir this over the stove-fire until the fruit is dissolved into a jam, and then withdraw the stew pan from the fire.

Roll out some trimmings of puff-paste, or else about half a pound of short paste, to the diameter of about eight inches, place this on a circular baking-sheet, and with the forefinger and thumb of the right hand, twist the paste round the edges so as to raise it in imitation of cording; then cut up a dozen ripe apricots into quarters, and place these in close circular rows on the paste, shake some sifted sugar (mixed with some rind of lemon) over the apricots, and then bake the tourte (at moderate heat); when it is done, pour the marmalade of apricots over the others, shake some sifted sugar mixed with a teaspoonful of cinnamon-powder over the surface, dish the tourte on a napkin, and serve it either hot or cold.

This kind of tourte may be made of every kind of fruit, the process in each case being similar to the above—consisting in baking one-half of the fruit on the paste, while the remainder is added after the tourte is baked, being first boiled down into a kind of jam for that purpose. In all cases, some cinnamon-sugar must be strewn over the surface.

Queen Victoria's chef Francatelli was trained in the complex Anglo-French system of nineteenth-century cuisine. However, after the marriage of Queen Victoria to Prince Albert of Saxe-Coburg, German food became fashionable at court. This excellent apricot tart is one of a number of German dishes that appeared in Francatelli's books. A sugar boiler was a copper pan with a small pouring lip. Unlike other copper saucepans it was not tinned inside, because such high temperatures were reached in boiling sugar that it made the tin melt.

JELLIES AND ICES

⚱ 196. ORANGE FLOWER AND PINK CHAMPAGNE JELLY ⚱

France 1828. (Carême, 231)

Clarify ten ounces of sugar, throw into it two ounces of orange-flowers, freshly picked, whilst the syrup is nearly boiling; cover it close, and when almost

*cold, strain it through a silk sieve, adding one ounce and a quarter of isinglass
and three quarters of a pint of pink champagne; finish as usual.*

Before commercially manufactured gelatin became available in 1870,
gelatins were made from various animal products rich in collagen. Calves'
feet, pigs' skin, immature stags' antlers, isinglass, and even ivory shavings
were all used. Of these, isinglass, or *col de poisson*, was the most favored
by high-class chefs because it did not have a gluey flavor. It consisted of
the dried and shredded swim bladders of sturgeons. Carême explains how
it was prepared for use by boiling an ounce and three quarters of isinglass
with two ounces of sugar in two quarts of water. This was skimmed of
impurities and allowed to reduce to half a pint. This quantity was enough
for one jelly. Nowadays isinglass is difficult to obtain, so you might have
to use a good-quality gelatin instead. The gray discolored sugar sold in the
early nineteenth century also required clarification before it could be used
to make jellies, which Carême insisted should always be transparent and
sparkling. Nowadays we do not need to clarify sugar, as it is already highly
refined.

If you want to replicate Carême's jelly but do not have isinglass, use the
following method. Soak 6 leaves of good-quality gelatin cut into shreds in 4
tablespoons of cold water for 20 minutes. Make syrup from 5 ounces of sugar
dissolved in 13 fluid ounces of boiling water. When the sugar has completely
dissolved take it off the heat and infuse in it an ounce of fresh orange flowers, or add a tablespoon of orange flower water when the syrup has cooled.
Dissolve the prepared gelatin in this. Cover until cool, add 7 fluid ounces of
pink champagne, and pour into a mold. Allow it to set in a cool place.

⊰ 197. MACEDOINE OF RED FRUITS IN STRAWBERRY JELLY ⊱

France 1828. (Carême, 234)

*Prepare the strawberry jelly as directed, and place the larger dome mould
upright in ice, fix the smaller dome within it, and fill up the space round
it with strawberry jelly. Pick twenty scarlet strawberries, and twenty white
raspberries, a dozen bunches of white currants, and as many red ones, wash
and drain the fruits on a napkin, handling them as little as possible; when the
jelly is firm, pour warm water into the small dome, and instantly lift it out;
place in the hollow thus left two spoons full of white currants, which surround
with a circle of strawberries, then a circle of white raspberries, and pour on
them a spoonful of jelly, and leave them to become set; continue filling up the
interior, by placing on the raspberries a circle of scarlet strawberries, then one
of the white currants, and so on to the top, occasionally pouring in jelly to set
them; to turn it out, dip it into warm water, take it out instantly, wipe the
mould and the top of the jelly, to prevent it slipping about in the dish; lay the
dish on the jelly, turn it over quickly, and lift off the mould.*

Macedoine mold with macedoine jelly.

A macedoine in this case is a mixture of fruits. Special macedoine molds were manufactured for making these elegant jellies. However, it is possible to achieve a similar effect without one. Pour a few inches of jelly into a decorative jelly mold. Let it set, then start building up your fruit in the center by sticking on a little at a time with some half-set jelly. Once this is firm, pour a little more jelly into the mold and let this set before you put in some more fruit. Continue this until the mold is full. Ensure that you put your strawberries and raspberries upside down in the mold, so they are the right way round when the jelly is turned out.

⚜ 198. ORANGES FILLED WITH JELLY ⚜

England 1845. (Acton, 436)

This is one of the fanciful dishes that make a pretty appearance on a supper table and are acceptable when much variety is desired. Take some very fine China oranges, and with the point of a small knife cut out from the top of each a round about the size of a shilling; then with the small end of a tea or egg spoon, empty them entirely, taking great care not to break the rinds. Throw these into cold water, and make jelly of the juice, which must be well pressed from the pulp, and strained as clear as possible. Color one half a fine rose color with prepared cochineal, and leave the other very pale; when it is nearly cold, drain and wipe the orange rinds, and fill them with alternate stripes of the two jellies; when they are perfectly cold cut them in quarters, and dispose them tastefully in a dish with a few light branches of myrtle between them. Calf's feet or any other variety of jelly, or different blancmanges, may be used at choice to fill the rinds; the colors, however, should contrast as much as possible.

The Victorian cookbook writer Eliza Acton borrowed this dish from Carême. It is rather time consuming but well worth the trouble. It is very easy to make with satsumas, as their flesh is easily removed from inside their skin. The oranges look particularly effective when filled alternatively with a white blancmange and a red jelly. Myrtle leaves are the sweet-smelling leaves of *Myrtus communis*. Use small fresh bay leaves if you cannot get them.

Orange jellies. Eliza Acton borrowed this recipe from Carême. This is his original illustration.

⚜ 199. ICED RICE PUDDING À LA CINTRA ⚜

England 1846. (Francatelli, 434)

Wash and parboil eight ounces of Carolina rice; then, put it into a stew pan, with a quart of milk and a pint of cream, two sticks of vanilla, twelve ounces of sugar, and a little salt; allow the rice to simmer very gently over or by a slow stove-fire, until the grains are almost dissolved, stirring it over occasionally with a light hand. When the rice is done, and while it is yet in a boiling state, add the yolks of six eggs; then stir the whole well together for several minutes, in order to mix in the eggs, and also for the purpose of breaking up and smoothing the rice. Let this rice-custard be frozen in the same manner as directed in the foregoing case, and then put it into a plain mould; cover it with the lid, and immerse it in ice in the usual way.

Molds for fancy iced puddings.

While the above part of the process is going on, a compote of twelve oranges (tangerine, if in season) should be prepared in the following manner: First, cut each orange into halves, remove the pithy core and the pips with the point of a small knife; then, with a sharp knife, pare off the rind and white pith, so as to lay the transparent pulp of the fruit quite bare, taking care to trim them neatly, and without waste; when the whole of the fruit is ready, throw it into a convenient-sized sugar-boiler, or stew pan, containing about a pint of syrup (made with one pound of sugar, and nearly a pint of spring-water), allow the pieces of orange to boil up gently in this for two minutes, and then drain them on a sieve. Boil the syrup down to about one-half of its original quantity; then, add two wine-glasses of Curacao, and three table-spoonfuls of apricot jam; mix the whole together, and pour it over the oranges in a basin.

When about to send the pudding to table, turn it out of the mould, and place it on its dish, dress the compote of oranges on the top and round the base, as represented in the wood-cut, pour the syrup over it, and serve.

The early nineteenth century saw the beginning of a craze for complex ice cream puddings, a fashion probably started by Carême. They often required elaborate molds, and pewterers vied with each other to produce new and fancier designs. This ice cream would first have been made in a *sorbetière* and then transferred to the mold. Any seams on the mold were sealed with soft lard. Then it was wrapped in brown paper. It was then plunged into a mixture of ice and salt. The lard prevented any salt from entering the mold and spoiling the ice cream. A covering of brown paper stopped pieces of ice from sticking to the mold.

APPENDIX: SUPPLIERS OF EQUIPMENT AND INGREDIENTS

Deborah Peter's Pantry. http://www.deborahspantry.com/index.html—Large range of period ingredients and some reproduction equipment.

The Sausage Maker Inc. http://www.sausagemaker.com/—Sausage casings.

Jas. Townsend and Son Inc. http://jas-townsend.com/index.php—Large selection of reproduction cooking equipment, including dutch ovens, cauldrons, some ingredients, and a range of useful cookbooks.

Richard Heinicke Ornamental Blacksmith. http://www.ranvilh.com/index.html—Excellent selection of iron cooking equipment such as trivets and fire irons.

SpitJack. http://www.spitjack.com/Merchant2/merchant.mvc—Range of clockwork spitjacks and other roasting and broiling equipment.

White Mountain Ice Cream Freezers. http://www.whitemountain-outlet.com/—Hand-cranked ice cream machines.

❧ NOTES

PREFACE

1. Antonin Carême. *Le Pâtissier royal* (Paris, 1815).

1. INTRODUCTION

1. *Le cuisinier methodique* (Paris, 1660), 8.
2. *l'Escole parfaite des officiers de bouche* (Paris, 1662), 128.
3. Antonio Latini, *Lo scalco alla moderna*, vol. 2 (Naples, 1692–94), 151.
4. Bartolomeo Stefani, *l'Arte di ben cucinare* (Mantua, 1662), 43
5. Robert May, *The Accomplisht Cook* (London, 1660), 150.
6. Edward Kidder, *Receipts of Pastry and Cookery* (London, c. 1720).
7. Selected from Latini, *Lo scalco*, vol. 1, 468–495.
8. From Stefani, *l'Arte.*
9. Emy, *l'Art de bien faire les glaces d'office* (Paris, 1768).
10. François Massialot. *Le cuisinier royal et bourgeois* (Paris, 1691), 285.

2. THE BAROQUE AND ROCOCO ERA, 1650–1750

1. Nicholas de Bonnefons, *Les delices de la campagne* (1654), 375.
2. John Evelyn, *Acetaria: A Discourse of Sallets* (London, 1699), 177.
3. William Rabisha, *The Whole Body of Cookery Dissected* (London, 1661).
4. From Louis Liger, *Le menage des champs et de la ville* (Paris, 1710).

5. Bartolomeo Stefani, *l'Arte di ben cucinare* (Mantua, 1662), 114.
6. Martha Bradley, *The British Housewife*, vol. 2 (London, n.d., c. 1770), 442.
7. From Robert May, *The Accomplisht Cook* (London, 1660).
8. Jean de la Quintinye, *The Complete Gardener* (London, 1704), 77.
9. Isaak Walton, *The Complete Angler* (London, 1653), 89.
10. Nicholas de Bonnefons, *The French Gardiner* (John Evelyn translation, 1658), 193.
11. *l'Escole parfaite des officiers de bouche* (Paris, 1662), 385.
12. From Louis Liger, *Le menage des champs et de la ville* (Paris, 1710).
13. May, *Accomplisht Cook*, 221.
14. Johann Georg Krünitz et al., *Oekonomische Encyklopädie*, vol. 188 (Berlin, 1773–1858), 446.
15. Vincenzo Corrado, *Il credenziere di buon gusto* (Naples, 1778), 20.
16. Antonio Latini, *Lo scalco alla moderna*, vol. 2 (Naples, 1692–94), 170.

3. THE REIGN OF LOUIS XV TO THE FRENCH REVOLUTION, 1750–1800

1. Apicius, *The Roman Cookery Book* (London: Harrap, 1961).
2. From *The Commonplace Book of Richard Hogarth* (Clifton, Westmorland, England, n.d., c.1770).
3. William Hall, *French Cookery* (London, 1836), 189.
4. From Vincenzo Corrado, *Il credenziere di buon gusto* (Naples, 1778).

4. THE REIGN OF NAPOLEON TO THE VICTORIAN ERA, 1800–1850

1. Eustace Ude, *The French Cook* (London, 1813), ii.
2. *l'Escole parfaite des officiers de bouche* (Paris, 1662), 128–132.
3. *Illustrated Times* (London, December 19, 1857), 427.

✥ BIBLIOGRAPHY

MANUSCRIPTS

The Commonplace Book of Richard Hogarth. 1770s. Private Collection, UK.
The Receipt Book of Elizabeth Birkett. 1699. Kendal Record Office, UK.
The Receipt Book of Elizabeth Rainbow. 1680s. Private Collection, UK.
English Receipt Book. c. 1677. Author's Collection.

BOOKS

Acton, Eliza. *Modern Cookery*. London, 1845.
Adam's Luxury and Eve's Cookery. London, 1744.
Agnoletti, Vincenzo. *Manuale del cuoco e del pasticciere di raffinato gusto moderno*. Pesaro, 1832–34.
Allerneustes brünner kochbuch. Grätz, 1791.
Altamiras, Juan. *Nuevo arte de cocina*. Madrid, 1745.
Apicius. *The Roman Cookery Book*. London: Harrap, 1961.
Appert, Nicholas. *l'Art de conserver*. Paris, 1810.
Audiger. *La maison reglée*. Paris, 1692.
Audot, Louis-Eustache. *La cuisinière de la campagne et de la ville*. Paris, 1818.
Beavilliers, Antoine. *l'Art du cuisinier*. Paris, 1814.
Bell, Joseph. *A Treatise of Confectionery*. Newcastle, 1817.
Benporat, Claudio. *Storia della gastronomia Italiana*. Milan: Mursia, 1990.

Bickelmann, George Conrad. *Lehrbuch der koch und backkunst.* Dresden, 1827.

Blegny, Nicholas de. *Le bon usage du thé, du café et du chocolat.* Paris, 1687.

Bonnefons, Nicholas de. *Les delices de la campagne.* Paris, 1654.

———. *Le jardinier François.* Paris, 1651. Translated by John Evelyn as *The French Gardiner* (London, 1658).

A Book of Fruits and Flowers. London, 1653.

Borella. *The Court and Country Confectioner.* London, 1770.

Bradley, Martha. *The British Housewife.* London, n.d., c. 1770.

Bradley, Richard. *The Country Housewife and Lady's Director.* London, 1727.

Brieve e nuovo modo da farsi ogni sorte di sorbette con facilta. Naples, n.d., c. 1690.

Briggs, Richard. *The English Art of Cookery.* London, 1783.

Brillat-Savarin, Jean-Anthelme. *Physiologie du gout.* Paris, 1826.

Caird, J. *The Complete Confectioner and Family Cook.* Edinburgh, 1809.

Calvacante, Ippolito. *La cucina teorico-pratica.* Naples, 1844.

Carême, Antonin. *l'Arte de la cuisine Française.* Paris, 1833.

———. *Le cuisinier Parisien.* Paris, 1828.

———. *Le maitre d'Hotel Français.* Paris, 1822.

———. *Le pâtissier pittoresque.* Paris, 1815.

Carter, Charles. *The Compleat City and Country Cook.* London, 1732.

———. *The Complete Practical Cook.* London, 1730.

La charcuterie ou l'art de saler, fumer, apprêter et cuire. Paris, 1818.

Clermont, Bernard. *The Professed Cook.* London, 1769.

Colquhoun, Kate. *Taste.* London: Bloomsbury, 2007.

The Complete Family Piece. London, 1736.

Il confetturiere Piemontese. Turin, 1790.

Cooper, Joseph. *The Art of Cookery.* London, 1654.

Corrado, Vincenzo. *Il credenziere di buon gusto.* Naples, 1778.

———. *Il cuoco galante.* Naples, 1773.

Le cuisinier gascon. Amsterdam, 1740.

Il cuoco Piemontese perfezionato a parigi. Turin, 1766.

Davidson, Alan. *The Oxford Companion to Food.* Oxford: Oxford University Press, 1999.

Di Schino, June. *Tre bancheti in onore di Cristina di Svezia.* Rome: Académie Internationale de la Gastronomie, 2003.

Dickie, John. *Delizia! The Epic History of the Italians and Their Food.* London: Sceptre, 2007.

Digby, Sir Kenelm. *The Closet of the Eminently Learned Sir Kenelme Digby, Kt. Opened.* London, 1669.

Dods, Mrs. Margaret. *The Cook and Housewife's Manual.* Edinburgh, 1826.

Dolby, Richard. *The Cook's Dictionary.* London, 1830.

Dufour, Philippe-Sylvestre. *Traitez nouveaux & curieux du café, du thé et du chocolate.* Lyon, 1685.

Duibuisson. *l'Art du distillateur et marchand de liquers.* Paris, 1779.

L'ecole parfaite des officiers de bouche. Paris, 1737.

Ellis, William. *The Country Housewife's Family Companion.* London, 1750.

Emy. *l'Art de bien faire les glaces d'office.* Paris, 1768.

l'Escole parfaite des officiers de bouche. Paris, 1662.

Etienne, M. *Traité de l'office.* Paris, 1845–46.

Evelyn, John. *Acetaria: A Discourse of Sallets.* London, 1699.

Fernández-Armesto, Felipe. *Food: A History.* Oxford: Macmillan, 2001.

Francatelli, Charles Elmé. *The Modern Cook.* London, 1846.

Gartler, Ignaz. *Nutzliches kochbuch.* Bamber, 1768.

Gilliers, Joseph. *Le cannameliste Français.* Nancy: 1751.

Glanville, Phillipa, and Hilary Young, eds. *Elegant Eating.* London: V&A Publications, 2002.

Glasse, Hannah. *The Art of Cookery Made Plain and Easy.* 4th ed. London, 1751. First published London, 1747.

———. *The Complete Confectioner.* London, 1760.

Grey, Elizabeth, Countess of Kent. *A True Gentlewoman's Delight.* London, 1663.

Grimod de la Reynière, Alexandre-Balthasar-Laurent. *Almanach des gourmands.* Paris, 1803.

Hagger, Conrad. *Neues saltzburgisches koch-buch.* Augsburg, 1719.

Hall, T. *The Queen's Royal Cookery.* London, 1709.

Hall, William. *French Cookery.* London, 1836.

Hamburgisches kochbuch. Hamburg, 1788.

Hammond, Elizabeth. *Modern Domestic Cookery.* London, 1817.

Howard, Henry. *England's Newest Way.* London, 1708.

Huber, Johanna Maria. *Bayerisches kochbuch für fleisch und fasttäge.* Stadtamhof, Germany, 1800.

Kettilby, Mary. *A Collection of above Three Hundred Receipts.* London, 1714.

Kidder, Edward. *Receipts of Pastry and Cookery.* London, n.d., c. 1720.

Kitchener, William. *Apicius Redevivus; or the Cook's Oracle.* London, 1817.

Kleine kölner köchin oder handbuch der kochkunst für bürgerliche. Cologne, 1846

Klett, Andreas. *Neues trenchir-büchlein.* Jena, Germany, 1657.

Krünitz, Johann Georg et al. *Oekonomische Encyklopädie.* Berlin, 1773–1858.

La Chapelle, Vincent. *The Modern Cook.* London, 1733.

La Mata, Juan de. *Arte de reposteria.* Madrid, 1747.

La Quintinie, Jean de. *Instruction pour les jardins, fruitiers et potagers avec un traité des orangers.* Paris, 1690. Translated by George London and Henry Wise as *The Complete Gardener* (London, 1704).

La Varenne, François-Pierre de. *Le cuisinier François.* Paris, 1651. Translated by I.D.G. as *The French Cook* (London, 1653).

———. *Le parfaict confiturier.* Paris, 1667.

———. *Le pastissier François* Amsterdam, 1655. Translated by Mounsieur (sic.) Marnette as *The Perfect Cook* (London, 1656).

The Lady's Companion. London, 1753.

Lamb, Patrick. *Royal Cookery.* London, 1710.

Latini, Antonio. *Lo scalco alla moderna.* Naples, 1692–94.

Lehmann, Gilly. *The British Housewife.* Totnes: Southover Press, 2003.

Lémery, Louis. *Traité des aliments.* Paris, 1702.

———. *A Treatise of Foods in General.* London, 1704.

Leonardi, Francesco. *l'Apicio moderno.* Naples, 1790.

Liberati, Francesco. *Il perfetto mastro di casa.* Rome, 1658.

Liger, Louis, Sieur d'Auxerre. *Le menage des champs et de la ville.* Paris, 1710.

Le livres de glace. Paris, 1845.

Lune, Pierre de. *Le nouveau cuisinier.* Paris, 1656.

Luraschi, Giovanni Felice. *Nuovo cuoco Milanese economico.* Milan, 1829.

Machet, J. J. *Le confiseur moderne.* Paris, 1803.

Manetti, Saverio. *Delle specie diverse di frumento e di pane.* Florence, 1765.

Marin, François. *Les dons de comus ou les délices de la table.* Paris, 1739.

Martin, Alexandre. *Le cuisinier des gourmands.* Paris, 1829.

Massialot, François. *The Court and Country Cook.* London, 1702.

———. *Le cuisinier royal et bourgeois.* Paris, 1691.

———. *Nouvelle instruction pour les confitures, les liqueurs et les fruits.* Paris, 1692.

Masson, Pierre. *Le parfait limonadier.* Paris, 1705.

Masters, Thomas. *The Ice Book.* London, 1844.

May, Robert. *The Accomplisht Cook.* London, 1660.

Menon. *La cuisiniere bourgeoise.* Paris, 1746.

———. *La science du maître d'hôtel confiseur.* Paris, 1750.

———. *La science du maître d'hôtel cuisinier.* Paris, 1749.

———. *Nouveau traité de la cuisine.* Paris, 1742.

Mollard, John. *The Art of Cookery.* London, 1801.

Moxon, Elizabeth. *English Housewifery.* Leeds, 1749.

Nebbia, Antonio. *Il cuoco maceratese.* Venice, 1786.

Nott, John. *The Cook's and Confectioner's Dictionary.* London, 1723.

Novo manual do cozinhiero. Lisbon: 1841.

Die Nürnbergische wohl unterwiesene köchin. Nuremburg, 1752.

Nürnbergisches koch-buch. Nuremburg, 1691.

Nutt, Frederick. *The Complete Confectioner.* London, 1789.

———. *The Imperial and Royal Cook.* London, 1809.

Nylander, Margaretha. *Handbok mid den brukliga.* Stockholm, 1838.

Parmentier, Antoine-Augustin. *Manière de faire pain de pommes de terre.* Paris, 1779.

———. *Le parfait boulanger.* Paris, 1778.

Paston-Williams, Sara. *The Art of Dining.* London: The National Trust, 1993.

Porter, John. *The Royal Parisian Pastry Cook.* London, 1834.

Rabisha, William. *The Whole Body of Cookery Dissected.* London, 1661.

Raffald, Elizabeth. *The Experienced English Housekeeper.* Manchester, 1769.

Ratta, Francesco. *Disegni del convito.* Bologna, 1693.

Rigaud, Lucas. *Cozinhiero moderno.* Lisbon, 1780.

Riley, Gillian. *The Oxford Companion to Italian Food.* Oxford: Oxford University Press, 2007.

Robinson, James. *The Whole Art of Curing.* London, 1847.

Rodrigues, Domingos. *Arte de cozinha.* Lisbon, 1683.

Salmon, William. *The Family Dictionary.* London, 1696.

Schellhammer, Maria Sophia. *Das brandenburgische koch-buch.* Berlin, 1723.

Shirley, John. *The Accomplished Ladies Rich Closet of Rarities.* London, 1687.

Die sich selbst lehrende köchin. Hamburg, 1803.

Smith, E. *The Compleat Housewife.* London, 1727.

Smith, R. *Court Cookery.* London, 1723.

Les soupers de la cour. Paris, 1755.

Soyer, Alexis. *The Gastronomic Regenerator.* London, 1846.

———. *The Modern Housewife or Ménagère.* London 1849.

Spencer, Colin. *British Food.* London: Grub Street, 2002.

Strong, Roy. *Feast.* London: Jonathan Cape, 2002.

Tarenne de Laval, G. P. *Le pâtissier a tout feu.* Paris, 1838.

Taylor, Elizabeth. *The Art of Cookery.* Berwick-upon-Tweed, 1769.

Thacker, John. *The Art of Cookery,* Newcastle, 1758.

Toussaint-Samat, Maguellonne. *History of Food.* Oxford: Basil Blackwell, 1992.

Townshend, John. *The Universal Cook.* London, 1773.

T. P. *The Accomplish'd Lady's Delight.* London, 1675.

Traité de confiture, ou le nouveau et parfait confiturier. Paris, 1689.

Trusler, John. *The Honours of the Table.* London, 1788.

Turquet de Mayerne, Sir Theodore. *Archimagaris Anglo-Gallicus.* London, 1658.

Ude, Eustace. *The French Cook.* London, 1813.

De verstandige kock. Amsterdam, 1669.

Viard, Alexandre. *Le cuisinier impérial.* Paris, 1806.

Vollständiges nürnbergisches koch-buch. Nuremburg, 1691.

De volmaakte geldersche keuken-meyd. Amsterdam, 1772.

Walton, Isaak. *The Complete Angler.* London, 1653,

Wheaton, Barbara Ketchum. *Savoring the Past.* New York: Touchstone, 1983.

The Whole Duty of a Woman. London, 1701.

The Whole Duty of a Woman. London, 1747.

Willan, Anne. *Great Cooks and Their Recipes.* London: Pavilion Books, 1992.

Wilson, C. Anne. *Food and Drink in Britain.* Chicago, Academy Chicago Publishers, 1991.

Wooley, Hannah. *The Queen-like Closet.* London, 1670.

Young, Carolin. *Apples of Gold in Settings of Silver.* New York: Simon and Schuster, 2002.

☙ INDEX

About the Author

IVAN DAY is a renowned food historian, museums and exhibitions consultant, and historic food educator, cook, and broadcaster in Cumbria, England. His 17th-century farmhouse houses his collection of antique kitchen artifacts and is the setting for courses offered on period food. Day's amazing work and passion are shown on his spectacular website, www.historicfood.com.

Recent Titles in
Cooking Up History